FOREVER

A

FIGHTER

By

Genafie Mcknight

ACKNOWLEDGEMENTS

I would first like to acknowledge and thank my heavenly Father. Because of his mighty and great works, this book is being published. He has diligently carried me out of the wilderness to His wonderful light. His grace and mercy over my life have been my lifeline and what has kept me.

Tonya, sister, I love you like no other. You loved me like I was your own. You provided for me without any questions asked. You had my back through all things and you have never forsaken me. Most importantly, you SAVED my life. Because of you, I am the woman I am today.

Imari, I'm beyond thankful for you. Your giving spirit, knowledge, competence, and love to help and encourage others to grow is astonishing. I have never met anyone that is as sincere as you. Your mission to see your people thrive is AMAZING!!!

Devantae and Mya Butler, thank you! Thank you for your submission to the Lord's calling over your lives. You two have fed me some spiritual meals, where I was able to become full and have leftovers for others. Moreover, your fire pushed me to walk into the calling the Lord has over my life. There are no words that I can express to thank you enough.

Pastor Ebony Moultrie, due to your obedience and answering the call over your life, God used you to minister, prophesy, teach, and love me in a manner that my soul needed desperately. Your transparency and vulnerability have helped me grow spiritually, in a mighty way. I sincerely appreciate you and love you abundantly.

Grandma Winnie, thank you for loving me and sheltering me as if I was your own. I'm happy you got to witness me prosper into the women I once told you I would become. Your love and dedication for me spoke volumes and I'm grateful that God placed you in my life.

Dr. DeMarquis Clarke, I thank you for being an educated African American man who walks with high levels of integrity and dignity. Your diligent in your treatment delivery and competent in your craft. Thank you for being transparent, down to earth and humorous personality throughout my treatment process. You challenged and encouraged me to transform into the women I desperately needed to become.

Nicole Narvaez Manns, thank you for bringing this book to life. I appreciate the hard work and dedication you put towards ensuring that my best work would be published.

Mickey Ellis, thank you for your help, guidance, motivation, and vision. Your kindness and enthusiasm pushed me to complete this book.

Contents

INTRODUCTION

How Did I Get Here?

Married, a four-month-old son, who was planned, a six-bedroom home, a new Tahoe, a great career, a Master's Degree from one of the top Universities, but here I sit, in the face of a therapist, weekly, crying my eyes out. Stuck in a mixture of depression, anxiety, obesity, heartache, trauma, and pain. From the time the therapy session began, until the walk back to my truck, I wiped tears from my face. I had everything any woman would want but I found myself in a space that I struggled very deeply to get out of. I questioned myself day after day, "How the fuck did I get here?" No matter what I had been through in life, and I promise you, I had been through hell and back several times, I had NEVER found myself in such a dark space or shall I say, I never acknowledged being there. I just wanted to, or so I thought, get back to the old me.

However, as Dr. Clarke helped me to look back at that

old me I wanted sooo badly to get back to, I began to acknowledge that the old me was also in a black hole. The old me always bounced back from shit and began to function, by normalizing and suppressing the pain endured. Week after week, each session would prove to me that the old me was not who I needed to get back to. I needed to actually go through a season of some deep healing to fully find me. I needed to find out who Genafie actually is; my purpose and who I am destined to be.

To get to that point, Dr. Clarke would walk me through my childhood and then right up to the point where I had sought treatment. He then brought everything together to better help me understand who I was and how to function at my fullest potential. So, I'll start from the beginning of how I actually got to this dark place.

CHAPTER 1

When the Trauma Began

"Good morning Toot and JJ." These two were my little brother and sister. They were all I had and I was all they had. In the morning, I would wake up and go to the kitchen, full of roaches, to prepare breakfast for us. At this time, I was around five and we were living in the Northview Heights projects on the Northside of Pittsburgh. The crack epidemic had hit the black community at alarming rates and my mother was one who had fallen victim to the madness. Our dads were not in the picture. My little sister and brother had the same father. I would find out years later that he was the one who got my mom to start doing drugs.

He was always caught between his addiction and jail. My dad was married and I would find out later that my mom did not know he was married until after she became pregnant with me . He was not in the picture either. Because of my mother's addiction, I tended to the needs of my younger siblings more often than not. Our older brother, Lavar, was five years older than I was and I do not have many memories of him ever living with us during this time. My mom would leave me and my younger siblings for hours at a time and I would make sure that we ate and that we were safe. Many times, we had very little food but would make it work by indulging in the food obtained from the community food bank. We would make the best of the cereal that would get soggy within minutes of pouring the powdered milk over it. Many times, we would eat the canned pork like it was a filet mignon, even though it smelled terribly. I can vomit right now thinking about it. We would go to town when the food bank would give out almost stale donuts. To soften them I would put them in the microwave and we would be in heaven. Oh and let's not forget about the syrup bread. At times, the bread would have mold on it but if that was all we had, I would cut the parts with the mold off, toast the bread and put syrup on it, as if we had five-star pancakes. This was our life. At night we would all cuddle together as if we were three peas in a pod. We were all we had.

Our life at the time was what many African-American kids were going through. Our mom always looked sad and unkempt. She always had people in and out of our house. I recall several men staying over our house. One early morning, I came downstairs to get us some breakfast and found her and a fully naked man on the pull-out couch. At times, she would leave us for hours at a time and other times she would entertain people at home. I had no idea what was going on from day to day. I just learned to survive and ensure that my siblings and I ate and that we stuck together.

During this time, my little sister and I became victims of sexual abuse. There was a set of twin boys, who lived in the row of projects behind us, whose mom would come to our house often and she would bring them along with her. Her sons were older than my little sister and I. On most occasions, when they would come over, we would all be told to go upstairs in the bedroom. Our moms would be downstairs, and we were told not to come down until they told us we were permitted to. During these encounters, the sexual abuse would occur. They would pull me and my little sister's pants down and sexually violate us. We had no idea what was going on. We did not know if what they were doing was right or wrong; we just laid there with them on top of us and stayed in the room until we were told we could come out.

At certain times, our mom would allow people to come and take us with them. I do not recall who many of these people were, but they would always bring us back home. One time, she allowed me to go with my uncle and while I was with him he bought me all types of snacks and I recall him taking me near some train tracks and meeting another man. I do not recall much after that but when I returned home, the area of my pants, where my vagina was located, had a hole in it. My mom immediately asked my uncle what had happened and he gave her some excuse. She knew something about my uncle and felt that he was not being honest, so she did not believe him. She immediately started yelling and crying. I had never seen her in that state before. She took me to the hospital to be examined. Again, I had no idea what was happening. Several doctors talked to me and pulled down my pants to examine me. My mom sat in the hospital with tears coming down her face. I do not know what came from that situation but my mom would not permit me to go with my uncle again, even though she would continue to allow other people to take us and bring us back home. However, one day, returning home didn't occur.

It was a summer day and I remember it like it was yesterday. My mom was sitting with me and my younger siblings on the couch, in the living room, and she was crying. She held all of us next to her as she wept. As she held us, a Caucasian lady came to our home. My mom had many people coming to and from our home, but never a white person.

While she allowed people to take us, none were ever white.

My younger siblings must have sensed that something was not right. As the lady told us to all come with her, my little brother and sister were not having it. They yelled, screamed, and tried to run back to my mom. We had no idea what was going on. My mom assured us that going with her would be fine and everything would be ok. I willingly went because I thought she was just another person taking us somewhere, but that we would come back home later. As my little sister walked to the car without a shirt and shoes, she would scream for my mom like never before. My brother cried too, as he walked barefoot to the car. I had to hold it together for them and comfort them because I had never seen them like this before. Although our mom stated everything would be ok, unfortunately, returning home would not happen at that time. I do not recall every moment, but what I do recall is walking to this individual's car. A white woman, a stranger, who ended up taking us to another stranger's house. We were taken to a lady's house and Oh was she mean! She took us to the store and apparently, we did not act according to her expectations, so she yelled at us and called us all types of names. This was just the beginning of repeated foster care placements. My siblings and I did not stay there long. The lady repeatedly yelled at me for taking care of my brother and sister the way that I did. She stated, time after time, that I was not their mom. I knew I was not their mom. I just helped them with everything they needed help with, but she did not like that at all. After a few days of staying there, the white lady, who took us from our house, came to pick us up. At this time, I got to know her name. Sally was genuinely nice to me and my siblings when she came and got us. She told us that we would be going somewhere else. I did not understand what was going on. I assumed that the lady was mad at me because I helped with my siblings too much and she did not like that. I thought we would be going back home with our mom but that would not be the case. Sally told us we would be going to another foster home. "Foster home, what is a foster home?" I questioned Sally. "A place where kids live until they can go back with their mommy," Sally explained. Confusion rose up in me because we were taken from our mom, but never told why. I wanted to like Sally, because she was nice to us, but I was also mad that she took us from our mom and I had no clue why.

Sally then took us all to separate foster homes. For some reason, we were all split up. My brother got dropped off first, then my little sister, and I would be last. I comforted them as they went to their new foster homes and told them everything would be ok, just like mom said. Each drop off consisted of us crying and not wanting to be separated, but that did not matter, because we were. The family loved me at the second foster home. They were all nice. There were several people who lived in the home and they all welcomed me and were so kind to me. My foster mom had two daughters and a special needs son that lived there and one of her daughters had a set of twin daughters who also lived in the home. The twin girls were so cute and had such long, pretty hair. My hair, on the other hand, was so tangled that I cried my eyes out when her daughter washed and conditioned it. Even with my nappy hair, they thought I was so cute and always said how pretty my eyes were. I enjoyed playing with the twin girls, because they were my age. I never had to worry about eating because I was able to eat all day and the food there was so good. My foster mom would cook dinner daily and it was never anything I ate when I was at home. No one would get on top of me at this home and I felt safe. I did not have to take care of anyone here and I actually got to be a child, even though I missed my little brother and sister desperately. Sally would come visit me and was always nice to me. She would even bring me stuff. I started to like Sally more and more, but I just always wondered why we were taken from our mom. I missed my mom and siblings so much. There were times that I would cry, but my foster mom would comfort me and tell me that everything would be ok. She would always give me snacks as a means to make me happy when I was sad and tell me how beautiful I was and how pretty my eyes were. On one of Sally's visits to the house I told her how much I missed my mom, little brother, and little sister. She stated that she was trying her best to find a foster home so we could be together again. In the meantime, she would schedule times for my siblings and me to visit each other. She would also set up times for us to visit with our mom. That brought me so much joy. Even though Sally never told me why she took me from my mom, this news superseded everything and from that point on and I started to really like Sally.

Visits with my younger siblings would begin. I would visit my little sister at her foster home and my brother at his. My little sister was always so meek and shy. She never really said much. She smiled and sucked her two fingers. Her foster mother was very nice. During my visits with my sister, I saw that her foster mom spoiled her. She knew my sister loved pancakes, with Mrs. Butterworth's syrup, and that is what she ensured my sister had whenever she wanted it. Every time I would visit, my little sister would run and show me her Mrs. Butterworth's syrup and all of the toys she was able to play with. I never had to care for my little sister when I would visit. We would always have lunch together and play. Our visits were so comforting to me, but as I would leave, she would become sad and we would cry. I did not visit my little brother much. I would primarily see him when Sally would pick us up to go visit with our mom. For months, our mom did not show up to any of the visits. Sally would pick all of us up from our different foster homes, take us to an office where we were to visit our mom, and our mom would not show up. I tended to handle the letdown well, but my little brother and sister did not. We would wait for about an hour before Sally would tell us she would be taking us back to our foster homes. My younger siblings would have total meltdowns, yelling that they wanted to see their mommy. I, in turn, would go into protective mode, staying strong, comforting them and telling them that everything would be ok, and assuring them that mommy would come and visit us soon. Sally would always take us to McDonald's to make us happy. I began to like Sally more and more, but as time passed, I missed my mom more and more. After a while, I started to dislike Sally for picking me up for visits because I assumed my mom would not show. I would then have to see my siblings break down and comfort them. After their breakdowns, I'd be separated from them until the next occurrence. Sally would do whatever she could to try to make us happy after every attempted visit we were to have with our mom, but it wasn't enough.

The first real Christmas I recall was at this foster home. The Christmas tree was so beautiful. Right before Christmas, during one of Sally's visits to the house, she brought me a few Christmas gifts. My foster mom said that I could not open them until Christmas day. I did not care because I was just excited that Sally had brought me some things. The entire home was decorated with Christmas decorations. My foster mom cooked so much food and baked so many cookies, pies, and cakes. She allowed me and the twins to help her bake the cookies. I remember waking up Christmas morning observing tons of Christmas gifts under and all around the tree. Some were wrapped and some were not. I had never seen so many gifts in my life and I was very excited about what I got, only to find out that very few of those gifts belonged to me. Most of the gifts belonged to the twins. They got all types of real Barbies, Barbie cars, a huge Barbie house, bikes, clothes, and shoes. They got ALL types of gifts. The smiles on their faces on Christmas day were like no other. The great thing is that they were so nice to me that they allowed me to play with their toys, so it wasn't like I really missed out on anything.

One day Sally came to the foster home. She was excited and happy to see me. She smiled happily as she told me that she thought she found a home for me and my siblings. She stated that she was taking us to the home that day to see it.

Sally's routine had always been to pick me up first and then my siblings and she followed that same routine this day. When my siblings got into her car I was happy to see them as always. They thought that we were going to attempt to visit our mom, but Sally allowed me to share the good news with them. That day was a good day. We had a good visit at the prospective foster home. She lived in a nice home and had an adoptive daughter who also lived in the home. Her adoptive daughter was a few years older than I was. Sally and the prospective foster mom talked and monitored us as we played together. The adoptive daughter seemed nice and played with us during the visit, but we would later find out things weren't as they seemed. There was a room full of toys and we really enjoyed ourselves. The prospective foster mom appeared to be genuinely nice and gave us all a hug before we left. She promised that we would be back to visit her home and said that she could not wait to see us again. The visit went very well and this was one time my siblings did not cry when Sally dropped them off at their foster homes. Her drop off routine consisted of dropping my siblings off first and me last. That day, I did not have to comfort them when dropping them off at their foster homes. This drop off was different. We were all actually happy. I told them that we would all be together soon and that I loved them. We would have a few more visits and then my younger brother, sister, and I were eventually all placed in the same foster home together.

CHAPTER 2

A Home Away From Home

Our new foster mother was an older woman who had 11 biological children and one adoptive child. Around this time, I was approximately six years old. All of her biological children were grown except for one and she lived with her father. I came to find out that her adoptive daughter was crazy. Our foster mother was a Jehovah's Witness and practiced her faith wholeheartedly. While living with her, we either called her mom or grandma. We were more her grandchildren's age and it felt more comfortable calling her grandma, but she acted in the role of our mom so we would also call her mom.

While living with her, she always had a house full of foster children. During those years, we would continue to have scheduled visits with our mom, but most of the time she did not show. We would be so excited to get dressed to go visit her, especially my little sister, and typically our hearts would be torn apart because she would not show. When she did show she would make false promises, show up with different men, and on one occasion she had a black eye. The times she did visit, she tried to show us that she missed us and always appeared sad. It then got to a point where the visits stopped and we would not see our mom for months and months at a time. She had the number to our foster home, but would only sparingly call. Our foster mom would always try to encourage her to get herself together because we were some beautiful kids. She would never say anything bad about our mom. My little sister's day would be so uplifted after a call with our mom.

We would go to court and she would not attend. We were forced to attend hearing after hearing, just to be told that we were not going back home with our mom. It would break my little sister's heart the most and at times she had her emotional moments, but most of the time she would remain silent, suck her two little fingers, twist her shirt, and smile.

The sexual abuse would continue as my new foster mother's adoptive daughter began to violate me and my younger siblings. The inappropriate sexual behaviors would continue to happen and this occurred basically the entire time we lived with her. No one, including Sally, ever talked to us about appropriate and inappropriate touching. Things occurred and we would all just keep it between us.

Our foster mother was not materialistic and when it came to clothes and shoes most of those things were covered by Children, Youth, and Families (CYF), who gave her a clothing allotment for us. We would get $150 every three months for clothing and shoes. Once we got under clothes, socks, a couple of outfits, and a pair of shoes, that $150 was gone. I hated the clothes that I had to wear. Her children were older, and they were very fashionable and I wanted the things that they had but she was not with that. She would not dare pay for a pair of Airmax shoes, because that would take almost the entire clothing allotment check. The most we would be able to settle for was a pair of cheap Nikes or Reeboks. Most of the time, Payless was where we got our shoes. She would end up keeping me and my younger sister for about six and a half years.

Everything at this home was strict and scheduled. We would attend the Kingdom Hall three days a week and were not allowed to play with what our foster mother would call, "Wordly Kids." Those were kids who were not Jehovah's Witnesses. She would always quote the scripture, "Bad associations spoil useful habits." We were allowed to go outside and play but were not permitted to go too far from in front of the house. Our lives consisted of going to the

Kingdom Hall, attending school, and playing in front of the house. She did not condone playing sports as she felt that sports took away from kids going to the Kingdom Hall and growing with Jehovah. She also believed that the kids who played sports were not Jehovah's Witnesses, therefore they were considered worldly. I do recall her signing up my siblings and me for swim lessons at our school. They took place every Saturday, but other than that, sports were a no go. As I got a little older, she permitted me to play with one of the neighborhood kids, Audie. Audie was an exceedingly sweet, kindhearted, compassionate girl. She did not live with her parents either. She lived with her grandmother. Their house was at the beginning of our street and I would be permitted to play with her a couple times a week. Audie's grandmother spoiled her and her grandmother always had snacks and stuff for us, so I really enjoyed going to her house and playing with her. She also had a swing set, sandbox, and fun toys to play with at her house and we really enjoyed each other's company. School was another situation. We really did not have any friends we hung with outside of school. Plus, I was in special education classes because my mom never took me to kindergarten, so I was a year behind in school. Additionally, my behavior in school was considered out of control; what might be considered hyperactive these days. My classes consisted of a small group of kids. The kids in my class were looked at differently from the other kids in the school. To complete assignments, I required one on one help and I recall how nice and supportive my special education teachers were. Each school year, I worked my way out of being in full-time special education to only needing help with reading and some math. One of my foster mother's daughters would purchase me books and when she would come over she would sit with me and have me read to her. She was so loving and kind. She adored me and always told me how beautiful I was. She always said I could come live with her. She had five children, but she treated me just like I was one of her own. She was so pretty, had a heart of gold, and was beyond kind. Her husband, on the other hand, was controlling and crazy. Even still, I enjoyed going to their house. Their house was beautiful and seemed to be located in the middle of the woods. We loved the nature walks and would see all types of animals while visiting. They had dirt bikes and motorcycles. We would make up all kinds of games and things to do there.

My brother was very hyper and was a daredevil at all times. On one occasion, he rode a Big Wheel down some hills, resulting in him running into a parked car and breaking his arm. I remember that day like it was yesterday. His arm was totally bent back. He yelled and cried like I had never seen before. He had a cast put on it and it ended up healing properly. On another occasion he was riding his bike and our neighbors' dog got off of the leash. The dog chased my brother down. He thought it was funny and for a while he did escape the dog, but I then witnessed the dog pull my brother off the bike and maul his leg. My brother laid in the neighbor's yard as I ran and got my foster mother, who called the paramedics and he was rushed to the hospital. He could not walk for a while, but thankfully, his leg eventually healed. The scars from that day remain visible down the back of his calf. To this day, I remain fearful of big dogs.

My brother lived with my sister and me for about three years before he was removed. He was placed elsewhere after someone in the neighborhood reported that he had done something he should not have and CYF felt he could no longer be in the same home with me and my siblings. My brother, however, never did anything inappropriate to me or my sister. He was placed in the East Hills Projects and we would visit him sometimes, but not much. He appeared to enjoy his foster home, but I missed him dearly when he was taken away from us.

One thing I'll say about my foster mother is that she kept me and my sister together and our needs were met. She was nice, loving and kind and we knew she loved us. On the other hand, she did not have a nurturing, motherly spirit. We never had mom-daughter talks; barely hugged, kissed or told each other we loved one another. She never discussed good and bad touches with us. If she had, we would have had an outlet to express things early on instead of living with her for six and a half years and nothing ever being discussed or disclosed. I believe her parental style was due to her age as she was old enough to be our grandma opposed to our mom.

Her children treated us well and my sister and I became a part of their family. After being in foster care for all of those years, a new law would pass causing us to be put up for adoption. My foster mother said that she would adopt me and my little sister. She was older so there was some talk about one of her daughters adopting my sister and one of her other daughters adopting me. The agency did not want us to be broken up and tried to locate a home that would take me, my sister, and brother but that did not happen. We went through the adoption preparation process and were informed that we would never be going back with our mom. Adoption photos were taken and a child profile was created so families could see and read about us to decide if we were children that they would want to adopt. A year went past and a family was never located. At this time, so many black families were broken and children were placed in foster care due to the crack epidemic,

21

that it was very difficult to locate a forever home for us. Our foster mother continued to inform CYF that she would adopt me and my sister. My mom, however, did not agree with us getting adopted. Although our foster mother informed my mom that she would permit continued communication and visitation between us, my mom was not ok with us being adopted. There was court hearing after court hearing and my mom refused to sign the adoption paperwork.

At this point, I was now 12 and I was sick and tired of going to court year after year, to be told we would not be going back with our mother. I was sick and tired of being told a home could not be located that would take me and my siblings. I was sick and tired of the entire process because up to this point, no one had ever told us why we were taken from our mom, it had been six years and we had barely seen her or why we were not permitted to go back and live with her.

We would attend another hearing and I was fully prepared to hear the same shit. A forever home had not been located and that we could not go back and live with our mom. However, this hearing was different. We had not seen our mother for a long time. We would talk to her sparingly on the phone, but had not had any visits for a long time. I would say approximately a year had passed from the last time we saw our mom. This day was quite different and we were shocked when the judge said, "You can go back with your mom." I have felt many things, but this was a time I can really recall feeling happiness deeply in my heart. I had not seen my mom for approximately a year, so to be told I would be going back with her was joy to my ears. Also, I had not seen either one of my brothers for years. I hadn't seen my little brother for over a year and I hadn't seen my older brother for over five years. Getting this news was what I was always desperate to hear and the words were finally stated!!

CHAPTER 3

Back to Survival of the Fittest

The plan was for my oldest brother to go back with my mom, then me and my sister, and then my little brother. Therefore, when my little sister and I went home, it was like meeting someone new, as we had not seen our older brother, Lavar, in over five years and had not lived with our mom for approximately six years. Moreover, he rarely visited or talked to her over the phone. We were excited that we were going back with our mom, but this was something new for us.

During this time, my mom lived in Mercer County, which is approximately an hour and a half from Pittsburgh. On the day we were dropped off with our mom, she sat on the couch in the living room area of the home and did not appear to be happy to see us. The home was an older home and was not in the nice condition of our foster home. It had an extraordinarily strong, unpleasant smell. After being home the first day, I realized the smell was due to the excessive cigarettes my mom smoked. My little sister was beyond excited to see our mom. She had always waited for this moment and she appeared to be in heaven. My mom had little food at the house, but we did not care; we were just excited to be with our mom. My mom stated that she would be going to get some food from the pantry the next day so we would have more to eat, but eating was the last thing on our minds. Being in the presence of our mom superseded everything.

Our brother, Lavar, was around 17 and did whatever he wanted to do. He had friends that he hung out with and he paid my mom very little attention. He did not go to school and never listened to any of my mom's directions. We saw him very little because he would come and go as he pleased.

Approximately a week or so after being placed back with my mom, the excitement about being home with her subsided. Living with her was totally different from our foster home. There was no structure or routine; we had little food or toiletries. It was far from what I expected and approximately two weeks after being placed back with her, I came to realize the reason we were taken from her in the first place.

One afternoon, it was thundering and lightning. Rain poured as we sat on the front porch. That day, my mom had gotten up very early. She had received her food stamps, was going food shopping, and stated that she would be back shortly. She returned later that afternoon with no groceries and as she walked on the front porch, I observed a crazy look on her face. The look in her eyes was far from normal; her speech was slurred and her body language unusual. She stated that she would be back and I immediately went into protective mode because I thought something was wrong with her. The look in her eyes scared me. I attempted to see what was wrong, but she was unapproachable. She basically blew me off and started to walk down the steps and down the street in the middle of a thunderstorm. I got my shoes on and ran after her, because I was confused as to what was going on with her. I became afraid for her. As I approached her, I began to cry and asked her to come back into the house. I begged her and told her that she did not appear well to me. She yelled loudly, as she pushed me away and told me to go back in the house. I sat in the rain crying because I had no idea what was going on. After a while, I became aware of what was behind this behavior. It was the drug that destroyed many black families: Crack. She had no control over her addiction and this behavior occurred regularly. Anytime she got her hands on any money she went and used.

After being returned to our mom, CYF remained

involved for approximately two months. The worker came to the house twice within that time frame. They came once, to bring our brother JJ to visit, and a second time to bring him to the house to live with us. For some reason, with all that was occurring, I chose to keep the secret about what was going on and stay with my mom, instead of disclosing and going back to foster care. Our brother was still the same hyperactive daredevil. He was always happy, but when he got mad, he would snap.

My mom's moods were often unstable. One day she would be nice and loving and the next day she would call me names like, "Funky, little Bitch." She called me every name in the book when she would get mad. She would also beat the shit out of me and my brother, JJ, when we failed to listen to her. The longer I lived with her the more I began to resent and hate her. Our foster mother never talked to us in that manner. Shoot, she never even cussed, let alone called us names. There would come a time when I would call my mom out of her name every time she called me out of mine.

The sexual abuse would continue. My mom failed to have any nurturing spirit within her. She never talked to us about what was and was not appropriate. Among my cousins, siblings, my mom's boyfriend, and aunt, inappropriate sexual behaviors were occurring regularly. Some of my older cousins and my aunt would all be in the attic of our home, drinking, smoking weed, and engaging in sex with one another. This inappropriate behavior was basically normalized. My mom would be on her crack sprees while this was going on. One time, she did get an overnight job and our house was considered the party house. On many days, my mother's boyfriend would sexually touch minor family members. Anger, rage, and resentment toward my mother came into play one night that she was out on one of her sprees. My adult cousin, who was drunk at the time, tried to forcibly have sex with me. At that moment I did not know what to do. Again, no one ever stated anything about sexual misconduct to me, so I was confused. Moreover, this type of behavior was basically normalized at my house. Yes, at 12 no one had ever told me that you were not to allow anyone to try to have sex with you, touch you in your private areas, touch anyone else in their private areas, nor engage in sexual relations with your family. I found out that family should not do such things when my aunt came to our house very upset because her daughter was allegedly having sex with my other cousin while my mom was not home at night. Overhearing that conversation led me to know that what my adult cousins were doing was wrong, but sadly, by this point, the activity was normalized because they continued to condone such behavior.

One positive thing I'll say about my mom is that she introduced us to church. She would ensure that we went to church every Sunday, even if she did not attend. This church's services were different for us because we had been raised as Jehovah's Witnesses for the previous six years. We would observe crying, running around the church, praising, and worshiping God and this was not what occurred at the Kingdom Hall. I was not sure if church was where her heart really was or if it was because she was sleeping with the pastor. My foster mom never brought a man to her home so to see my mom with a man who was married and a pastor, at that, was very discouraging. My mom would not interact with the pastor inappropriately at the church because the pastor's wife would always be present. However, I would witness my mom interacting with the pastor inappropriately when he would come to our house. My mom would then attend church like nothing had happened between them. She would even interact with his wife while at church.

My mother introducing me to church was the best thing she could have ever done because I loved everything about it. I enjoyed attending, loved participating in the youth choir and youth activities. There was something about church that drew my heart to love it and to worship God. The church would also help us with food and household things when my mom would sell her food stamps, resulting in us not having food or toiletries. The corner store would give her food on credit and she would pay her balance with her food stamps when she received them. So between paying that balance and selling the remainder, many times we lacked food. On some occasions, she would buy food that she would end up selling to get money so she could use drugs. The church and local food pantry would be our source of food and household items on many occasions.

Christmases would become a factor once again as we were no longer being raised as Jehovah's Witnesses. My mom did not have the funds to get us anything for Christmas, but she made sure to sign us up for donated gifts. For our first Christmas at home, a rich white couple sponsored me and my siblings. They came to our house on Christmas Eve and provided us with all with an abundance of gifts. The following Christmas, we would get sponsored again. My sister got sponsored in a major way that year. She got hundreds of dollars' worth of things and many Barbies. She loved everything she got. My brother and I also received a lot of things, but not as many as my sister. The day after Christmas we would wake up to nothing. Everything was gone. My little sister's heart was broken. All she wanted was her Barbies, but my mom made up an excuse about someone stealing the stuff. She was not aware that I figured out that she sold the things that we had received. Christmas night I observed her from the upstairs window taking bags of stuff out of the house. I put everything together once we came downstairs the next morning and the gifts were gone. I did not mention what I knew to my little sister. She just sat there looking sad, while sucking her fingers, twirling her shirt, quiet, but she would still smile if you said something to her.

Around this time rage, anger, hate, hurt, and continuous pain continued to build up in me. I started to hate my mom more and more. My cousin would continue trying to forcibly have sex with me. He would pull me onto his lap or get on top of me with a hard dick and I would always fight him off of me. At this time, I was thirteen and he was around twenty. This was not the life I expected, but for some reason, at that time, I would rather stay with my mom than go back into foster care.

Right before I turned 13, I started my period. My mom had never talked to me about this. I started bleeding and was fearful, so I told my aunt. She, in turn, told my mom. My mom taught me very little about proper hygiene when I came on my period. Furthermore, many times we lacked pads so all of my underwear became ruined. My aunt showed me how to use toilet paper as a pad. Around this time I had been back with my mom for a little over a year and she had purchased me no new clothing, underwear, shoes, or socks. Nothing new at all and all of my clothing became too small or ruined. She would go to the local food pantry, because it was also a second-hand store, to attempt to get me used underwear and clothing, but much of the clothing was too big for children. Therefore, I had no choice but to wear my older brother's clothing. I would walk around, looking like a boy, in his baggy pants, that could fit me and three other people. He would get mad because sometimes I would ruin his clothing.

I started attending a new school, but did not make many new friends. It was a predominately white school, so there were very few black kids. There were about two other black kids in my classes and they were both wealthy, so I did not interact with them much. Most of my time in school, I misbehaved because I did not want to be there. I was embarrassed to be dressed like I was. Moreover, my everyday life at home always had my mind in other areas while I was at school.

We would go without light, gas, and water. I hated it there but for some reason I still did not want to go back to foster care. When we did not have water, we would fill big jugs of water up from our neighbors' hose. Someone must have called child welfare on us because a worker came to my school and questioned me about our water being disconnected. I lied and stated that the report was false. When we did not have lights, we used candles and we learned to heat up water to wash in the sink when we did not have gas. We did not have a washer and dryer so we would wash the little clothing we did have in the sink and hang dry them. In the winter time there would be many times when the morning would come and my clothing would still be wet. I would iron them dry. When our iron broke, I would open the oven door and hang the clothing from the stove area and when the one area was dry we would turn it over so the opposite side would dry.

I began to want to know about my dad so when my mom was in a good mood, I would ask about him. She told me his full name and told me that she met him when she was working at Coo Coo's jitney station, on the Northside of Pittsburgh. She said he was a drunk and had a lot of kids. He was married when she got pregnant with me but she told me that she did not become aware of that until after she had me. He was also much older than she was, by about 20 years. I was anxious about getting to know him but also wanted to be saved from what was going on at my mom's house. I took it upon myself to look him up in the phone book and shockingly, I found him. Anytime I would get a hold of a phone or some change to use the pay phone, I would secretly call the number listed in the phone book and a woman would answer. She would always say he was not home. I would then ask her to tell him I had called. I did this for a year. I even sent my school pictures with a letter attached to the address listed in the phone book but never received a response. One day I called, and the women answered but did not say he was not home. She told me to hold on. At that very moment I got nervous and after speaking with him, I felt a pain that would live with me for years. He got on the phone and in a very agitated, angry voice he said, "Stop calling my house. I am not your dad." He then hung up. That would be the last time I would ever call his phone again. I never told my mom what happened, and I never asked her about him again.

For some odd reason, with all the turmoil that was going on in my living environment, I still did not want to go back to foster care. I was, however, tired of living the way we did, so at 12 I got a newspaper job and babysat to make money for us to eat and so I could buy things for myself. I did not make much money from either job but the little I did make; I was able to make stretch. This was the beginning of my doing whatever was necessary for us to eat. We ended up getting evicted from our home and had to move to the local subsidized housing complex. It was a new school district that had more black kids. I automatically made new friends. Most of the kids were going through what I was facing so we all clicked. At this time, I was around 13 years old and weed had become my best friend. I drank a few times but did not like it as much as I liked being high. It eased my racing thoughts and daily pains.

My mom continued to be verbally, emotionally, and physically abusive. She said many hurtful things. She said she "fucking hated" me, she called me "Bitches", and an "ugly motherfucker" too. You name it, she said it. She would beat the shit out of me and my brothers with anything she could get her hands on. One day I got so mad because of our poor living conditions, her wanting to get high instead of taking care of us, and her calling me names. She started calling me a Bitch and with anger in my heart, I called her a Bitch in return. She then decided to beat me with a bat, causing my eye to be black for a month. The schoolteachers and CYF questioned me and again I lied and said that my brothers and I were playing baseball and I was accidentally hit with the bat. Again, I could not find it in me to tell the truth. For some reason I did not want to go back to foster care. For the first time, my Mom had remorse for what she did. She looked me in my eyes, cried, and said, "I'm sorry. I did not mean to do that."

However, the abuse continued.

I started to stay over my neighbor's house often. School let out for the summer and my mom decided to move back to Pittsburgh. She took my two younger siblings. My older brother was 18 so he was out living somewhere that I do not recall. Our neighbor, Fawn, had a baby and I would babysit him. Fawn then allowed me to move in with her and I stayed in her basement. She was always high and happy. She smoked weed 90 going north. Often, I would take the smoked down joints that she left lying around and she never guessed I was smoking her weed because she thought I was a good girl. Fawn allowed me to stay with her that summer. She was loving, kind, and real. She clearly loved to have sex because almost every day I would hear her and her boyfriend having sex. This older guy, who lived not too far from Fawn, said that he thought I was pretty and that he liked me. At 13, I enjoyed knowing that someone like me. We would talk on the phone and hang out by Fawn's house. Not soon after hanging out with him, he too would try to have sex with me. One day as I was babysitting for Fawn, and he came over to hang out. He asked to come in the house, and I permitted him to do so.

On the living room couch he would forcibly attempt to have sex with me, but as he tried to penetrate me, I was trying to fight him off me. As I was fighting, he stopped because he heard Fawn and her boyfriend about to come into the house. I did not tell anyone about this, but I made it clear that he should never call me again. He would call the house a few times after that incident, but I would not talk to him and eventually he stopped calling. I stayed with Fawn for about three months and I do not recall what prompted it, but my mom said I had to come to Pittsburgh.

We began to stay with my grandmother in the St. Clair Village projects. I began to drink more often and also started to smoke much more than before. I met some friends and outside of school, all we did was smoke weed and hang with boys. I had a nice body and many boys tried to talk to me. Older guys tried to pursue me even more than the ones my age. After all of the sexual trauma that I had endured, I refused to even consider talking to anyone who approached me in a sexual way. The boys I hung with gave me the accessibility to smoke and drink, so I hung out with them regularly, but having sex with them was a no go. As I would walk down the street, so many older men would whistle and yell, "Damn, you got a fat ass!" These remarks were such a turn off. Sex was the last thing on my mind.

My mom continued to get high, but my grandma made sure there was food and household toiletries. I looked much older than a 13 year old, because I had hips, a big butt, and a very small waist. Many of the individuals who sold drugs to my mom touched me inappropriately and I was often able to fight them off of me. Ever since I overheard that conversation between my aunt and mom, I knew what they were doing was wrong. Even though I was dead set against having sex with them, I begin to engage in other risky behaviors, such as holding their drugs and guns in the basement of my grandma's house, where we were staying, in exchange for weed and money. I also began to make money babysitting people's kids. Around this time, our utilities were always on because we lived in the projects. My grandma moved out and allowed us to remain at her place. Food became scarce, clothing was at the bare minimum, and household items were always in short supply. Therefore, the money I was making was to ensure me and my siblings were good. My mom just thought I was babysitting, but had no idea of the other things I was engaged in.

CHAPTER 4

Becoming a Product of My Environment

A t this point in time, I was in my early teens and I was basically living an independent life. The drug use got really bad with my mom. Darn near every woman that was my mother's age was on crack and my siblings and I continued to suffer. I do not recall ever going to see the PCP, eye doctor, or dentist the entire two years I was back with her. I was very mature for my age and my main focus was on making money to survive. I believe that helped me, but also hindered me. Due to my mature nature I came across several women who were in their early 20's and had their own housing project. I became a popular in-house babysitter. At times, I would be babysitting seven to eight kids at a time and they would pay me. That was the way I continued to eat, drink, and purchase what I needed to soothe my mind. Most of them smoked weed and I had full access to take their leftover weed when they were not looking and some of them even smoked with me. With the money they paid me, I would buy weed and go to the beer house and purchase beer. One night I got very drunk after consuming an entire 40 ounces of St. Ides beer. I threw up everywhere. My brother, JJ came in the room and knew something was not right. He put it all together once he smelled the vomit, which of course smelled like beer. I recall being so drunk that I could barely turn on my side to throw up. He threatened to tell, but as always, my mom was running after her addiction so she was totally unaware of this incident. That entire summer I stayed at someone's house, babysitting their kids.

I met FeFe through watching the kids of a girl named Toney. Toney and I lived in the same housing project. FeFe worked the overnight shift and her boyfriend was a truck driver. She asked me to babysit her kids while she worked and she would pay me. She put the baby-sitting check in someone's name, but stated she would pay me the money once she received it. I stayed with her for approximately two months, babysitting and taking care of her kids. During this two month I would go to the house and check on my sister and brother regularly and make sure they had food. I recall the routine my foster mom had us on and I implemented that with her kids. She would leave in the evening and return the next morning. I was responsible for cooking the kids' dinner, ensuring that the house was clean, and putting the kids to bed. She allowed her younger cousins to come over her house and stay. At this time, I developed a crush on one of her cousins. I was 13 and he was around 16 or 17. He was way more advanced than I was and quite used to saying what was necessary to get into girls' pants. His whole motive of trying to entertain me was to take my virginity. Since I was naive and never had anyone talk to me about boys, I fell for what he would say. I thought he liked me as much as I liked him, but that was not the case. As I lay on the bathroom floor of FeFe's home as he penetrated me and took something from me that should have been a special moment, I felt nothing but pain. I wanted to force him off of me like I did everyone else that tried to have sex with me, but I liked him and that is what he wanted so I did not fight him like I did everyone else. As he finished, I gathered myself together, went upstairs, got into the bed and cried. FeFe must have sensed something was not right because she called shortly after I went upstairs. One of the kids brought me the phone and said she wanted to talk to me. She asked me if everything was ok and I told her that it was. I then fell asleep and he came into the room and penetrated me once again. I liked him but I damn sure wished someone would have had the conversation with me about sex because that is not what I anticipated. That experience not

41

only traumatized me but put me in such a mindset that I would not have sex with anyone else until I was 18 years old. The next day would consist of him telling his younger brothers and friends about what he did. It was a glorious moment for him to brag about taking my virginity. My usual routine continued as I babysat FeFe's kids. Nights when they would go to sleep, I would go outside and sit peacefully and smoke my weed. Weed was my best friend. So much consumed my mind but that was the only thing that calmed me and gave my mind some peace. No raging thoughts, the internal anger would cease, and peace would come upon me.

When it was time for us to return to school that fall, FeFe paid me about two hundred dollars. I was pissed because I watched her kids for two whole months and she only paid me that small amount. I needed school clothes, my hair done, shoes, and underwear and two hundred dollars was not cutting it. I did not say anything because that was a place for me to stay and I ate there daily. I took the two hundred dollars, caught the bus to Gabe's, a discount store, and made that $200 stretch. I was happy to finally go to school on the first day, with a new pair of Nikes and a nice outfit. FeFe did do my hair for school because she did hair on the side. She eventually asked about me and her cousin and I initially told her nothing was going on. She then told me that she had read my journal and was aware of what happened, so I told her the truth. The next day, when I got to school, CYF was there to pick me up. I do not know if FeFe called them, or if the school did, but a worker came and told me I was going to a group home.

"Fuccckkk!!!" is all that went through my head. I asked about my brother's and sister's whereabouts. I was informed that my little sister went with her dad and her paternal siblings and my brother went with a foster family. Again, we were all split up. I was able to talk to both of them on the phone. My sister was happy because she was with her dad. My brother was with a Christian family, who had sons and other males his age. He appeared to be happy where he was placed. I, in turn, was put into a fucking group home with girls who all came from tough backgrounds, so fighting, hate, and maliciousness was what consumed that place. I became so fucking angry at my mom. I felt that I had endured so much stuff over the first 14 years of my life because of her addiction. The hate for her really began to flare more intensely as I laid each night in that group home. I recall spending Christmas there without my family, but instead with girls feeling the same hurt that I was enduring. Although the staff tried to make the day fun and happy, we all sat there fucked up in the mind. I could not see my siblings or spend time with my family. New Years' Day in

1998, I recall looking out of the window of that group home with my eyes full of tears. Asking myself why I had to live this type of life. "Why don't I have a family like most kids do?" I promised myself at that moment that when I had children, they would never face the shit I had at such young age. I stayed in that group home for approximately six months and those months in that place caused the hate for my mom to grow at an extremely high rate. The feelings for my dad remained buried, as he was never around, so in my mind, I dismissed him mentally, but as I grew older, I longed for his presence. I can say that I ate daily, had clean clothes, had all necessary toiletries, could shower daily, and had a clean place to sleep. However, the environment was toxic and no child should have to live in such conditions because of their parents' issues. Other than the one staff member, Ms. Betty, who was extremely funny and cool, I fucking hated every minute of being there. I could not smoke to ease my mind and daily fights and arguments with the other girls would occur.

My court hearing was coming up and my caseworker called me and asked if there was any family that would take me and I said I did not know. She asked if there was anyone I knew that would allow me to live with them and I mentioned my old foster mom, Ms. Winnie. She stated that she would investigate that and get back to me. When she initially looked into it, she said that Ms. Winnie only took younger children, not teenagers, but the foster care agency she worked for was going to contact her and see if she would make an exception and take me back. My caseworker called me back and said that Ms. Winnie agreed to take me back under certain circumstances and she then went through her long list of rules. I had to wait to go to court so the judge could grant permission for me to go with Ms. Winnie. During the waiting period, I talked to her daily. She was encouraging and said that she was happy that I mentioned her name, because she would always be willing to take me back. She adamantly informed me of her household rules and having to attend the Kingdom Hall with her three times a week. At this moment in my life, I was willing to agree to anything in order to get out of this group home. At my next hearing, my brother moved with my grandmother and I went to Ms. Winnie's home. I went from an extremely chaotic lifestyle, to a quiet home, in a decent neighborhood. I tried my best to be a part of sports and find a place that would hire me at 14. I hated going to the Kingdom Hall, but I went because that was a part of the agreement in order for me to move back into her home. I attempted to stay busy with sports and school because those were ways that I could get out of going to the Kingdom Hall.

The only downfall with sports was that I had to find a friend who was also participating because she would not take me or pick me up from practice or my games. So when I played basketball and ran track I would get rides from my friends' parents. I was going to a predominantly white school and most of my teammates' parents where highly involved and attended their child's sporting events. I rarely had anyone in the stands to support me. I could have been great at basketball but had no one to invest their time in me to teach me the skills and offer me support. Smoking weed and drinking ceased as I was not in the projects, where I had easy access to it them.

At 14, I was able to get a summer job and at 15 I was able to start working at Wendy's. When I started working there, I stopped participating in sports. I would rather work to get the nice shoes and clothes everyone else had, as opposed to playing sports. My foster mother did not care about me being a teenager and wanting to be in style. The only clothing that she was willing to purchase was from the clothing allotment of $150 every three months. What would

$150 dollars buy a 15-year-old growing, young woman? Every week, I worked the maximum number of hours that I was permitted to work. Additionally, no one would ever come to see me or support me at my games and it was hurtful after games, to see my friends go and hug their parents and hear their parents discuss how great they did or offer comfort when we lost. I, on the other hand, sat back and visualized this and became more and more angry with my mom and by this point, anger towards my dad begin to surface. Hate and rage started to consume my entirety.

When I got my first summer job, Ms. Winnie required me to open a bank account and put $50 out of each check into my account. She also offered to get a cell phone on her account, but I had to pay the bill when I got paid. During this conversation about money, I expressed how I felt. I did not get smart with her but I did say that it was my money and I should be able to do what I wanted with it. Since she did not buy me clothes and shoes, I wanted to use my money on those things. I also expressed that I did not feel that I should have to pay my cell phone bill when she received a monthly check for me. She went on to say that the check was for household expenses. Her response stunned me because she would have had the same household expenses whether I lived with her or not. Monday through Friday, I ate breakfast and lunch at school and worked at least four days out the week. When I worked, I ate there. Therefore, the grocery bill was not that much, and the lights, gas, and water did not increase that much from me being there. I then stated that I could not wait until I became an adult because I was going to open a home and get teenage foster girls and take good care of them. I said that the check I got for them would be used strictly on them. She stated, "Yeah, that is what you say now."

After this conversation, I felt God speak to me for the first time. He made it clear that I would write a book and my book would be turned into a movie. I would get a PhD and operate a foster home for teenage youth. At that moment, I was very confused by this. I did not like to read or write, so publishing a book was not something I would even consider at the time. The next day, I dismissed the revelation of writing a book and obtaining a PhD but openly and proudly went to her and stated, "I am going to open up a group home for teenage girls, but not like the ones they have now. It's going to be a home that shows them so much love, so they do not have to feel like I did and I'm going to use their whole check on them." She smiled and stated, "Ok, we'll see."

At 16, I wanted to obtain my driving permit and my foster mother took me and I passed on my first attempt. However, she would not permit me to use her car to practice driving. When I attempted to go through a driving school to learn how to drive, there was something in the CYF stipulations that would prohibit me from doing so.

But there was a bright spot. The manager at my job, Angie, offered to teach me how to drive. Once she realized I had it down, she allowed me to use her car while she was at work; I simply had to put gas in it. Ms. Winnie did not know of this. I could drive well, but I could not seem to master parallel parking.

I was not really permitted, but I somehow managed to start hanging out with certain kids in the neighborhood. This was my way of sneaking and smoking weed with them. I was with Ms. Winnie for about six months before I started smoking weed again to cope. I had little contact with my siblings. I was hurt because I was in foster care and they were both with family.

I had rekindled friendships with peers I had previously built relationships with prior to going back with my mom. My behavior in school was not great. I got suspended several times, but never failed a class. On one occasion, a girl called me a nigger and I beat her down in the cafeteria. Ms. Winnie had warned me if I got suspended or acted out again, I would have to leave her house. During this time, my loyalty to my friends was strong. One girl started messing with a guy who was dating one of the girls I hung out with. The girl and I got into a verbal altercation in school and it resulted in us fighting when we got off the school bus. I did not get suspended for that fight because I had gone into the house first to pull my hair up and to take my bookbag in. Since I went into the house before we fought, the school did not have grounds to suspend me. However, that was not sufficient for Ms. Winnie. She put in her 30 day notice for me to be removed from her home.

Right before leaving Ms. Winnie's house, my life was spared for the first time. Through my journey, God has spared my life on four occasions but the initial time was at Ms. Winnie's. One day I was picked up early from school because I was ill. I was never sick, so she thought I was faking until she came to the school and saw my condition. When I got to the house, I sat in the living room chair and started to fall asleep. Stomach pains hit me and increased to the point that I had to lay on the floor in a ball, as a means to comfort myself. Ms. Winnie had left to go to the store, so I was at home alone. As soon as I lay on the floor, I heard the window shatter and a loud noise. I was in so much pain that I could not comprehend what occurred. I had to get up off the floor because glass had shattered onto me. As I got up, I observed that someone had broken the window, but I did not understand how as I did not see anything but broken glass on the floor. As I turned around, I observed a hole in the wall and automatically knew someone had shot into the house. It is amazing that I would lay on the floor the moment I did because if I had not, I would have been shot in the head. The bullet hole was right behind the wall of the chair I had been sitting in.

Because of Ms. Winnie submitting a 30-day notice for me to be removed from her home, CYF attempted to locate appropriate family members, but prospective family was not appropriate or did not wish to take me. CYF then located a foster home for me and that woman was the devil himself. The only good thing about that arrangement was that I was back in Pittsburgh and was able to see my siblings more. I transferred to the Wendy's location by the new foster home. I worked the maximum amount of hours permitted. When I got off of work on the weekends, I would go to visit my sister or my cousins. I had all of the access and freedom to smoke weed again. My cousin was around 18, had her own project housing, and lived close to my new foster home so I would visit her regularly. Around this time, my little sister was living between her paternal sisters, Kesha and Tonya. When I would go visit, Tonya treated me as if I too were her sister. I loved her personality and she was very open with me.

Feelings of distress would often consume me because my siblings were with family and I was not. I had not talked to my mom in about a year and did not know what she was up to. I hated the foster home I was living in. My caseworker continued to ask me about finding someone in my family to take me. I would often visit my two cousins who were around four to five years older than I was and they had their own place so I could smoke as much weed as I wanted as a means to ease my mind. They were too young to take me in, plus they both had two children of their own. My mother's sisters had taken in my aunt's nine kids so they did not have room for me. The only person I could think of was my grandma. The CYF worker called her and she bluntly stated she would not take me and basically asked the worker to stop asking her. She stated that I was out of control and she was not dealing with that. I was confused by her statement because I worked and went to school daily and never failed a class while in high school.

My foster mother was terrible. She did not buy me clothing, household items, nor food, and was not supportive. She made me seem like an outcast to CYF though. She had the audacity to portray to CYF that I never talked to her, but only stayed in my room when I was home. Fucking right I stayed in my room! She did not take care of me, nor give two shits about me so why would I want to talk to her? When the CYF worker would come to the home to visit me, I would sit and listen to what the worker and my foster mother had to say and expressed the bare minimum. I would continue to remain in my room whenever I found myself having to be in the house.

One time, I had a long day of school and working at Wendy's, getting cussed out by drunken college students. I did not have the opportunity to smoke on my walk home and I was beyond irritated. When I got in the house all I smelled was crack. As I entered the house, the smell of crack consumed me. I had to walk past my foster mother's bedroom to get to mine and the odor got even stronger as I walked up the steps and towards her room. At that moment rage consumed me. I went into my bedroom and fucking cried because I was so mad. When I heard her come out of her room, I confronted her and she then started to call me all types of names. She was high as a fucking kite and she had the same look in her eyes that I had seen when my mother was high. I looked her in her face and expressed every bit of anger that was in me. "How the fuck can you sit here, smoking crack when you do not buy food, pads, razors, the soap I use, soap powder, deodorant or lotion and you question why I do not leave my room when I am in this fucking house? I pay my own cell phone bill and take care of myself when you get a check to provide for me and do not do a damn thing for me. Like How??? I fucking hate you and I want to get out of this house!" She replied that no one wanted me and then bluntly looked me in my face and stated, "Bitch, you'll never be shit." At that moment I lost it. I charged towards her room and she shut her door. I went into my room and began packing my things. I called Tonya, hysterically yelling and crying. I begged her to come and get me. I never felt this broken before and I knew I did not have anywhere to go. No one in my family would take me and I damn sure was not going to call my grandma, the only person who had the space to take me but very clearly stated, on many occasions, that I was not welcome at her house. I got as much stuff as I could grab and I ran out of that house with tears running down my face, with rage and anger like never before. I wanted to beat the shit out of that lady. How do you talk to a child, that you are paid to care for, like that? How can an adult, who is supposed to care for and support you, be the individual that caused further trauma? From that night on those painful words would be the ones that would replay in my mind over and over, "Bitch, you'll never be shit." Those hurtful words gave me the power and strength to work extremely hard and to accomplish every dream I had ever imagined.

CHAPTER 5

She Saved Me

That night, Tonya immediately came and got me and took me to her house. I cried during the entire ride to her home. She promised that everything would be ok. I did not want to go back to that group home and no family would take me. She told me over and over again that she would do whatever she had to do and everything would be just fine. This would be the first time someone stated that everything would be ok and it actually turned out to be ok.

Tonya had two sons that were younger than I and she also had a fiancé. She talked to CYF the next day and they permitted me to stay with her. At 16 and a half I was finally placed with a family that was healthy. There were no drugs being used; the home was in a nice neighborhood; Tonya and Frank were incredibly supportive, and they took great care of me. They really showed that they loved me and this was something that I had never experienced before. They both worked in the healthcare field and had decent jobs. CYF told them that they would have to go to foster care classes in order to get a check for me. They attempted to go, but with their busy schedules they did not get the training done within the 60 day time frame that they were given, so CYF stopped their check. My social worker came to the house and told them that the check would be stopped because they did not complete the training within the designated timeframe. Tears filled my eyes because I thought I would have to leave since the check stopped. Tonya looked at that lady and stated, "Ok, she will be fine because my fiancé and I work and we do not need the check." For the first time in my life, I finally felt secure living with Tonya. She did not know everything that I had endured, but she was open and honest with me. Her rules were to go to school and make passing grades. I could work if I wanted to and I could hang out with friends, as long as I was home by curfew. If I wanted to stay over a friend's house, I needed to call and get her permission and I did everything she expected. I lived with her from 16 and a half until I was 18 and a half and she taught me so much in those two years. The time with Tonya would be the steppingstone toward not becoming a product of my situation. During that time, she and Frank took great care of me. If I was involved in anything, they supported me. I always had the newest Airmax and Jordan footwear, as well as name brand clothing and my nails and hair were always done.

Although I was in a great home, all of the childhood pain and trauma lived inside of me. My mind would take me to places that brought painful memories. I continued not to have any contact with my mom. Many times, I would become overly sad for no reason. So, I would use my comforter, which was weed, daily, to ease my mind and the painful memories would cease. I continued to work at Wendy's and attend school. I met two females Chell and Shawnell and they would become my best friends. Shawnell some weed and Chell did not. I also hung out with another group of friends and we all smoked and drank. Tonya did not know I smoked weed and although I smoked daily, I respected her enough not to come home looking or smelling like I had been smoking. When we would go out, she would see how guys would look at me. I had the tiniest waist, a butt that basically sat on my back, and these beautiful hazel eyes. Tonya schooled me on boys and what to do and what not to do. Her relationship with Frank showed me how a man should treat a woman. She spoke to me about her mom being on drugs and how she had made it and was now a nurse. She expressed how she was a single mom going to nursing school, while having two kids and how she was able to graduate. She made it clear to me that I could be and do anything that I wanted.

The most important thing that she stressed to me was the difficulty of taking care of her children while she was a single mom and how important it was that I was upfront with her when I thought about starting to have sex. She stated that she would want me to get on birth control when that thought came to my mind and I promised to let her know. Her drive for success gave me drive. I told myself that no matter what I had to do, I was graduating from high school. At this time, no one, from my grandmother to my generation, had graduated from high school. All of my cousins, who were older than I, had dropped out of high school. Most of them had at least one or two children. I was the next in line to graduate and I promised myself I would do just that.

The first time Tonya got upset with me was when she took me to get my driver's license. I failed because I could not parallel park and I acted a pure fool at the DMV. She got angry with me but not how others had in the past. She yelled, but did not once call me out of my name. She did not threaten that I would have to leave her house because of my behaviors, and she encouraged me not to ever act in such a manner again because it was totally unacceptable. She told me that ladies do not act like that. By that evening, she was no longer mad at me, but told me she refused to take me back out there because what I did was not cool. Frank took me out there and I failed a second time. I got upset and he laughed and told me to cut it out. The third time, I passed and he was as happy for me as I was for myself. Frank was like the father I never had. He was genuinely kind; never looked at me in a sexual manner; worked hard, and cared for me as if I were his child.

Tonya schooled me on so much, especially sex and relationships. Around this time, Julian and I had been dating for almost two years and started to have conversations about sex. Before we were to have sex, during a ride in Tonya's car, I shared my thoughts with her. We made an appointment for birth control the next day and she made sure I made it there. One thing about Tonya was that she made sure that I was schooled about boys and what to do and what not to do. I had bought Julian a pair of Timberland boots for Christmas that year and she made me take them back. She said that you never buy a man shoes because he will walk out of your life with them on. He was pissed, but I listened to her. Julian and I would sneak and have sex while his mom was at work. We would leave school early, so I would be gone before his mom arrived home. For homecoming, Tonya allowed me to stay the night at Julian's house. She said that as long as I was open with her, things would be cool. Julian's mom loved me so she too was open to the idea.

Julian and I dated until the end of my junior year in high school. It was like I was more mature than he was and we just grew apart. That summer, Chell's brother, Aaron, tried to talk to me. He was about three years older than I was. We talked and went out often. He also smoked weed, so that was one thing we did every time we hooked up. He was totally different than Julian because he was older and more experienced. He was also in the streets and messing with him drove me to have an attraction to street guys. After dating him for a few months, we became intimate and I loved having sex with him. His maturity, experience, and vibe had me gone.

Tonya did not attend church, but she talked about thanking God and would listen to gospel music that would bring a feeling into the home that was calming. I thought about church and God often, but between school and working, my time was darn near taken up.

After a year of living with Tonya, she decided that she was leaving Frank. This would be around the end of my junior year of high school and at this time I was 18. I did not understand the reasoning because everything seemed so good. Frank was such a great father figure to me and her two boys and I really could not understand why she was leaving him. She was planning on moving out of the home he had purchased for her and into a two bedroom apartment. This would be the first time I would get upset with her because I did not understand what he did for her to be leaving. Why would you move from a home that he bought you to a two-bedroom apartment? Although she stated that I could move with them, a two bedroom was not going to cut it for me and her kids. Therefore, I felt the need to find my own place because I refused to go back to a group home or live uncomfortably in anyone else's home.

My CYF worker tried to beg me to stay in the system and told me that they would find me somewhere to live until I graduated, but I refused. I had an entire year left of high school and continued working. I then tried to plan out how I would be able to work, go to school, and maintain my bills if I got my own apartment. My CYF worker referred me to an independent living worker who loved me and treated me like her daughter. Ms. Regina always went above and beyond for me. She explained to me how difficult it would be to maintain an apartment, work, and go to school, but I was adamant. She provided me with a list of reasonably priced apartments. I told Tonya my idea and she reminded me of all of the bills that I would have to maintain, in addition to going to school. She told me to think about how I liked to buy clothes, every pair of Jordan's, and Air Maxes. She was straight forward with me and stated that working at Wendy's was not going to cut it.

Tonya said her job was hiring certified nursing assistants and told me that I could be hired because I was 18. Therefore, that summer consisted of me taking CNA classes, Monday through Friday from 7:30 am to 3:30 pm, for six weeks. Attendance was a huge requirement. Every morning, I was up a little after 5 am and was on the 6:15 am bus headed downtown. I would then get on another bus, which would get me from town to the training location within 15 minutes. Aaron would also take me to work on nights I would stay with him. I did that for the entire six weeks and did not miss a class. I passed every written and clinical test and graduated. Tonya had to work, so no one attended my ceremony, but I was beyond happy that I had completed it. I was paid $10 an hour while completing the training and $12.50 an hour once I started working. I had six months to pass the state exam. I failed the initial time because I did not have the scale properly centered during the test, resulting in me failing that part of the exam. I rescheduled the exam and passed. I thought I was making major money being able to earn $12.50 an hour, plus an additional two-dollar shift differential because I worked the 3 pm-11 pm shift. My addiction to weed continued and I would smoke before work and on my lunch break. However, soon enough, work would also become a strong addiction. Between school and work, I remained busy, so I did not have time to even entertain any hurtful or traumatic thoughts. I worked, went to school, and smoked during my free time.

While working there I met Kathy. She became like a good friend, but she was about ten years older than I was, so I identified her as my aunt. She smoked weed heavy and I would smoke with her often when I got off work. Kathy was also cool with Tonya. At this time Tonya was unaware that I smoked weed until one day Kathy slipped up and said something. Tonya immediately got upset and looked at Kathy differently because she felt Kathy was way older than I was and should not be condoning such behavior. On the other hand, smoking was my comforter and eased my mind, so I hooked up with Kathy quite often.

CHAPTER 6

Made it So Far for the Moment to be Taken from Me

A bout a month into my senior year in high school, Tonya had moved into a two-bedroom apartment with her boys. Frank did not tell me I had to leave, nor did he say it was ok for me to stay. Therefore, I really felt pressed to move into my own place. When Tonya initially moved, I did not have my own place, so Aaron allowed me to stay at his apartment until I found a place.

I ended up finding out that he had a girlfriend, which I discovered one day when I went to his job and she popped up there. He would constantly lie about dealing with the girl and would tell me that he wasn't. That entire three weeks of staying with him I really did not feel safe because he sold drugs and the woman he was dealing with could show up as she pleased. He assured me I was cool and that she could not get into his apartment building because she did not have a key. He also continued to deny that he was messing with her and that she was obsessed with him and kept coming around. When I got off work, he would be at his apartment waiting to let me in and most times would leave back out to "hit the block" as he would say. He would come in late, shower, have sex with me, and sleep until it was time for me to get up and go to school. He made sure I attended school every day.

One day, the woman showed up as we were going into his apartment. He took me inside and then went back outside and talked to her. He came back in shortly and apologized for her showing up. He made sure I was cool and saw the hurt on my face. That was one night he did not go back out and hit the block, but stayed and held me all night. He continued to apologize and told me he loved me and that it would not happen again. He was the first guy to say that he loved me. I believed that he loved me because he allowed me to stay with him, would make love to me and made sure that I went to school and work. I honestly believed he loved me but at the same time, the search for my own apartment became top priority. I found an apartment within the next few weeks and paid to move in early. I continued to deal with him but once I got my own place I never stayed at his apartment again. He would run between me and his girlfriend. I was young and dumb and would believe whatever he said to me.

My rent at the time was $450, plus I had to pay for food, light, gas, cable and my phone bill. My bills added up to around $850 a month. I rarely cooked because I was never home, due to my school and work schedule, therefore, I ordered out most evenings, while at work. Without overtime I brought home around $750 every two weeks. After paying my bills I had around $900 to spare. By the time I bought my weed, paid to eat out almost daily, and bought the new Jordan's or Air Maxes that came out, I was broke.

My entire senior year consisted of going to school from 7:15 am until a little after noon. I had a half day of school because I had all my credits and verification that I worked. I would then leave school to work from 3 pm to 11pm. When I got off of work, I would catch the bus home and do it again. Most of my weekends consisted of me working sixteen hours shifts which included me working 3 pm to 11 pm and then 11 pm to 7 am Friday, Saturday, and some Sundays. Mondays were my worst days because I would get off at 7 am, get a jitney home, get a shower, and then get a jitney to school. I would get to school late but it was cool because my first period was my study hall.

I worked extremely hard my senior year of high school to pass all my classes, to work to maintain my bills and to get the things I wanted for prom. I wish I had the opportunity to play basketball, run track, and play volleyball with the excitement of my parents cheering me on in the stands. Those memories were just thoughts that brought sadness to my soul. I did not have the luxury to participate in such activities because I was forced to work and surviving was my priority. I would hit the clubs on the weekends when I did not pick up overtime. I would use my cousin's ID to get into the club. At the time I really did not drink much; weed was my comforter.

Many days Aaron would come to my place because he was running between me and the other girl. I was 19 and she was about 24. She would call my phone asking me for him and questioning why I was messing with him. She would ask me if I was pregnant or tell me that she had heard that he bought me things. My entire senior year, I allowed him to do this. On my free days he would take me out to dinner and the movies. He would buy me things and always told me he loved me. No one ever said they loved me so when he stated that to me it took my thoughts about him to another level. I felt that he really loved me but his actions contradicted the words he spoke. One day he and I got into an argument and did not speak for a few days. So I called his phone and the girl answered and she questioned me as to why I was calling his phone, knowing he had a girlfriend. I told her that he continued to tell me that they were not together. We exchanged words and I informed her that he stayed at my house several days out of the week and that he had a key to my house. She then told me that I was stupid to give a dude with a girlfriend a key to my place and that they would be on their way to my house to return my key. He showed up with her in the passenger side of the car. I went outside with the biggest knife in my apartment to stab this bitch but this old bat would not get out of that car. He did not look at me but handed her the key and she in turn handed it to me. I could not believe this dude had the audacity to bring this bitch to my house and I was furious. She would not get out of the car because I was ready for her. I could not believe I was a senior in high school, arguing over a dude, with a 24 year old woman, who still lived with her mom and dad. How the fuck was this occurring, especially about a dude who said he loved me? My own dad had never said that he loved me. No man had ever said they loved me and he did and I could not understand how he had the balls to do what he just did. I called his mom and my best friend hysterical. His mom took me under her wing because she knew I was young and my mom was not in my life. She knew what her son was doing. All she heard was me yelling and crying, but she couldn't calm me down. I was alone in my apartment and did not know what to do and felt like I lost a part of me when he did that disrespectful shit.

His mom called me a jitney and told me to come and stay at her house until I got myself together. I cried the entire night about that shit. I went to school the next day, but called off of work, stayed home, cried, and smoked weed that entire day. I wish I could have said that was the last time I dealt with him, but it was not. He would come and apologize and say how sorry he was, but at that point I believed nothing he said. His mom told me straight out of her mouth to leave him alone. I did not immediately disconnect from him, but I no longer believed anything he said to me. The girl would continue to call and play on my phone. When he bought me things, it would get back to her because he would ask me why I was running my mouth about what he does. The rumor then came about that I was pregnant by him. She called my phone about that. The shit I went through dealing with him was crazy.

I went to Schenley High School and that school was known for the female students being fly. Prom was the word of the town every year. Everyone got their outfits made for prom and after everything that was taken from me, I refused to miss prom. I ended up getting my prom and after prom outfits made and made sure that I made hair and nail appointments with the best stylist in Pittsburgh and pulled up with the best ride, which was a stretch hummer. As I worked, I paid everything off.

Something amazing happened that really helped me stay on top of my bills and pay for prom. One day, I went to the ATM to withdraw money from my account. There was about $2000 extra dollars in my account. I immediately went into the bank and inquired about where the money had come from. They informed me of the source and gave me a number I could call to inquire about the transaction. I called the number and was informed that it was accumulated child support from my dad. When I was in CYF care, the child support went to the state to cover my costs of being in foster care. When I left, the money had been accumulating and they were able to locate my bank account via my social security number and deposited the money into my account. I would continue to receive the support until I graduated high school. This dude had been paying child support the entire time I was in foster care, but when I called he stated he was not my dad. How in the world did he live his daily life knowing he had a child that he had not seen for 19 years? Just how? That shit hurt my heart bad. My mom put a drug before me and my dad just basically did not give a fuck about me. My heart was filled with so much hate for my mom and everything I had been though because of her addiction, but at that moment the hate for my dad sat right beside the hate I had for her.

After working hard all school year, prom came around

and that was a very exciting thing for me. I stopped dealing with Aaron, but he would call my phone often expressing how much he missed me. I had everything in place for my prom. I was so proud of myself. I paid $3,500 all by myself for prom so I was ready to show out on that day.

Around this time, I really did not communicate with my mom and my father remained non-existent to me. I was able to beg my mom to come to my house to see me off to the prom. She did not seem happy for me at all, but she never did. She said I looked beautiful, but never really showed how proud of me she was. At prom, people were ecstatic about my stretch hummer. As we drove past everyone, all I heard was, "Who is in that?" I stuck my head out of the sunroof and who did I see? Aaron's girlfriend! I immediately became upset and said, "Yeah, this is how I do, old ugly bitch." We continued to drive off, but had come to a stop light so I stuck my head out of the sunroof, excited and dancing. Aaron's girlfriend was in the back seat of her friend's car and as her friend sped past my stretch hummer, his girlfriend spit at me. The spit did not touch me but at that moment a rage I never felt consumed me. She did not know how hard I worked for this moment. She did not know the long hours I worked to get where I was and this bitch spit at me. I wanted to kill that bitch and I promised myself that I would make every attempt to locate her to beat the dog shit out of her. I also promised to beat her sister's ass, because she was in the car hyping her up.

That Monday after prom, I went to her neighborhood looking for her and I found her. She was driving down Herron Ave in the passenger side of her friend's cars. I jumped in the street and told her to get out. I beat the brakes off of her. Slammed, punched and stomped her until her friend tried to break it up. As I had her in the head lock punching her she started to bite the side of my stomach. The harder I punched her the harder she bit me. I had to pick her up and slam her in order for her to let loose. I knew that she had taken a chunk of my flesh off of me. As she sat on the ground, I continued to punch and kick her. I wanted to see blood and I did not care what consequence I would have to pay. As she sat on the ground getting punched, her friend tried to give her a bottle to hit me with but that was an epic fail because my friend took the bottle and threw it. About four people had to grab me off of her. She got up and ran to the car and tried to pull the door shut. I ran after her and pulled the door open, spit in her face, and said, "Bitch, do not ever spit at me again." Her friend came over to the car and tried to pull off as I tried to pull her out the car because I was not finished getting out my frustration. She was able to shut the door and as her friend pulled off, she yelled out the window,

"That's why you don't have a mom." I grew even angrier. This old, immature bitch had the audacity to say that, but I had to admit that it was the honest truth. I was 19, with my own apartment, as I finished high school and this girl was around 25 still living at home. After fighting her I would coincidently see her sister walking down Penn Ave. My friend Tia and I were on our way to hang out at her house. I stopped the car and said to Tia, in a very relaxed manner, that I would be right back. I was going to beat her ass real quick. Tia was so confused because my demeanor did not match my plan to fight. Tia asked, "Genafie, are you serious?" I calmly got out of the car and rolled up on her and beat her ass in the middle of Penn Ave. She said that she did not want to fight me and had nothing to do with me and her sister. I said, "You two were yelling out of the window when your sister spit so you are getting it too." Who would know she also liked to bite people? As I stomped her, she bit my leg but I had pants on so it did not hurt as much as when her sister bit me. I beat her up, threw her purse in the middle of the street, called her and her sister cannibals, got back into the car, and then went to Tia's house like nothing occurred. Tia was like, "What the fuck just happened? You really calmly got out of the car and beat her up." From that moment on, I told myself, if a bitch looks at me wrong, I'm going in on them.

Being tired, angry, and irritable consumed me. After prom, I had to go back to class and finish my senior project and finals. I was extremely burned out as I continued to work a lot to stay up on my bills and the things that I wanted. Who would have thought that I would get into an argument with the principal and he would state I could not walk at graduation? I had worked an 11 pm -7 am shift, went to school, was beyond tired, and got into it with the principal. I said some things that should have never come out of my mouth and in turn, he said I could not walk at graduation. What the fuck? My independent living worker tried to advocate for me, but it did not work. The principal stood his ground. I can honestly say that I said something to him that I do not wish to repeat, and he had all rights to discipline me, but taking away the graduation ceremony was going too far. I did not have parents that would go to the Board of Education to advocate for me. The principal did not know what I had just faced at prom a couple weeks prior. He didn't know that I would be the first of four generations to graduate high school or that I had worked 16 hours, three days straight, to turn around and come to school to complete my graduation obligations. Because of all of the circumstances that I was facing, I was under such high levels of stress, causing me to snap at him. He was the coolest principal I ever had and showed how much he really cared about the students. I had no right to disrespect him like I did. He felt that I had gone to the extreme with my actions but I thought the same thing about him. I could not believe this shit. I would be the first out of four generations to not only graduate high school but also without a baby and I could not participate in the ceremony. I had paid for my cap and gown and as I picked it up I had hopes and prayers that the principal would change his mind, but he did not.

I decided not to attend graduation, but my best friend's mom talked me into still going with her and sitting in the stands with my cap and gown on. She had also bought me a dress and some shoes to wear to graduation as a way to get me to attend. As I sat there, so much hurt and pain consumed me. Neither my mom, nor my dad was present. Actually, the only individuals that came were my previous foster mother and her daughter.

The school would permit individuals to participate in graduation even if they had credits to still complete as long as they were enrolled in summer school to complete the needed credits. I, on the other hand, actually did everything to graduate and had all the required credits but could not walk across the stage and had to sit in the stands and watch individuals who were not getting their diploma, get the joy of walking across the stage, as their family yelled with joy. What a fucking joke. I worked hard for prom and graduation and they were both ruined. As I fought to break a generational curse, I was broken and shattered into pieces. That summer I went to all of my friend's graduations parties but did not have one for myself. I was the first out of four generations to graduate and not one individual thought to throw me a graduation party; not even my damn mom.

CHAPTER 7

Continued Patterns of Unhealthy Relationships

R ight after high school, I registered for classes at the local community college. I stayed at my job until about a month after I graduated high school and was fired because of my unprofessional work behavior. I was 19, working with a lot of older, irritable women and would politely inform them that I would beat their ass if they ever came at me sideways. I finally fully left Aaron alone, but he would continuously call my phone and pop up at my job and house. Once I was done, I was done and did not want any parts of looking back. Plus, he had a baby with that girl so I really did not want anything to do with him.

One night, a couple of girls I hung out with, who lived on the Hill, called me over so we could drink and smoke. On a typical day I would hook up with them, but I was so high that I fell asleep and never went over to hang out. That night, a drive-by shooting would occur and one of the women got shot. This would be the second time that God had spared me. I was not going to church around this time, but when I got the call about her getting shot, the first thing that came to mind was if I had gone and chilled with them, that could have been me. My best friend, Shawnell was into all types of stuff. She connected me with some guys and I started doing illegal things for them. I then started this pattern of involving myself in extremely risky behaviors. At least once a week, I was driving to New York and New Jersey for them. They would give me a thousand dollars every trip so that helped me with my bills and prevented me from having to work overtime. My little sister remained a huge part of my life and around this time she had two kids. I would help her when she needed assistance with birthdays or holidays. I was coming across so much money and did not know how to manage it, so I was blowing thousands of dollars like crazy, on material stuff, weed, trips, my nails, and hair. I remember going to a car auction by myself and buying a car. Someone broke into my house and car and of course I did not like that, so I stopped dealing with the guys I was driving to and from New York and New Jersey for. I would meet other guys and would be their ride to get around and I made money off of that; all while I continued working as a nurse's aide and attending college.

I then dated a guy about 14 years older than me. He sold weed so that was easy access for me to smoke. Plus he looked out for me financially but once he crossed me, I automatically dropped him. My heart became hardened and I did not allow anyone fully in and I did not open up to anyone. The angrier I got, the faster I would eliminate people out my life.

I started a new nurse's aide job not too far from my house. Coincidentally, while working there I met the owner of the jitney station that my mom told me had previously employed my dad. I asked him if he knew my dad and he said that he did. He said I looked just like my older sister and had hazel eyes just like my dad. He said that he and my dad had hung out, had a lot of women, and drank a lot back in the day. He said that my dad lived in North Carolina and came to visit him a couple times a year. I worked there for about two years and became very close with Choo Choo. He always gave me words of encouragement and told me to stay in school and reach for the stars. He was like a dad to me. He knew I was in college and lived out on my own and told me how pretty I was and how much I had going for myself. When I worked, he would always ask for me to take care of him or if I was not assigned to him he would ask the staff to tell me to come to his room to help him. Most times, he just wanted me to keep him company and I would do that until he would suddenly start snoring.

One day, as I sat at the nurse's station, charting, he called me as he typically did. He was sitting there with a man that I had never seen visit him before. I went over to Choo Choo and he looked at the man and asked him, "Joe, do you know her?" and the unknown man responded, "No." Choo Choo then stated, "Her name is Genafie and that's your daughter." His faced dropped and he turned around away from me, as if he was in total shock. I smelled liquor on him and when he spoke, it confirmed that he was drunk. He turned back around and said, "Genafie." Since he was intoxicated, the conversation was not of any length. He asked me for my telephone number and said that he would call me. My anger for him elevated to a higher level. I was 19 years old and my father did not even recognize me and that senseless conversation left me speechless. This was the same man who told me to stop calling his house, saying that he was not my dad, but as I looked in his face, I saw a strong resemblance. I looked just like this man.

I continued to smoke weed, but drinking became more prevalent. I did not know how to cope with the things in my life so I began to drink more and more. I also did not understand the importance of college life, since no one in my family had gone before. I would go to bars with my cousin's ID and drink. That became a routine of mine. I would make sure that I went to class and worked but when I got off at 11 pm, I had a blunt rolled and was at someone's bar drinking, at least four days out of the week.

One day, while sitting in class, I received a call from a long distance number. For some reason I had a feeling it was my dad. I walked out of class and answered and a man asked if it was Genafie and I said that it was. He then stated, "This is your dad." He sounded drunk. He said he wanted to call and see how I was doing and wanted to see me soon. I told him I was in class and he said that he would call me back later, but he never did. I called him a few times but never received an answer. A few months later, I became aware that he was not doing well and was at the VA hospital. I called the hospital and they connected me to his room. He did not sound well or happy to hear that I was calling. I then went to the hospital to see him and he appeared upset and angry. A woman was there with him and later I found out that she was his wife. I did not stay long because I did not feel welcome there. I left with hurt in my heart. About two months would pass and Tonya called me to tell me that someone called her and told her that my dad had passed away. She said that he passed at one of my sister's homes and gave me the address. I went to the home and a woman answered the door. I introduced myself to her and told her who I was. She looked me dead in my fucking face and in the rudest and angriest voice, asked me where I had been all this time. I looked at her with a blank stare and thought to myself, "Where the fuck has my dad been all these years? I was in foster care and struggling to become a productive woman!" My dad's body was still at the house when I arrived. I looked at his dead body and did not even think to cry.

My dad must have informed them about me because they told me that they had just recently become aware that I existed. I later found out that the lady who answered the door was my sister and she was his favorite child. I became aware that my dad had 13 children, which consisted of two from his first marriage, six from his second, and five outside of his marriage, with different women. His favorite child also said that she did not think it was appropriate to put the names of the children he conceived outside of his marriage in the obituary. My oldest sister, Rhonda, took to me to the side and said she was not having that. When she found out who I was, and that I had been in foster care my entire life, she broke down and cried. She said that her children were my age and that she would have taken me. She stated that they had no idea I existed until recently. Prior to my dad dying, he told them all of the kids he had, and my name was on the list. Rhonda took my number and promised that she would call me. I was not going to attend the funeral, but Rhonda encouraged me to attend. As I sat in the church, on the day of his funeral, at the age of 21, all I thought of were the five encounters I had with this man called my dad. During the call when I was around 12, at the nursing home when we first met, when he called me while I was in class, when I saw him at the hospital, and now viewing his lifeless body. These five, fucking non-meaningful encounters are the memories I will forever have to accept and live with. I could not even cry at the funeral; I was more pissed than anything. After the funeral, my sister Rhonda would continue to maintain contact with me and tell me how much she wanted to build a relationship with me.

I started to drink more and more. After my first year of college I decided to go to the Marines and make a life out of that. I gave all of my clothes and shoes away because my plan was to leave within the next couple months. Tonya needed a bigger place, so instead of me having to break my lease, she moved into the house I was renting. After about a month of trying to get my urine clean from smoking weed and trying to lose weight, which was unsuccessful, I decided not to go to the Marines. I remained angry and would get into arguments with the supervisors whenever they said anything to me. The drinking and smoking would continue and the more I did that, the worse my grades got. After a year of college, I ended up not registering for courses the following fall. I partied like a rock star. I went to spring break in Daytona Beach, Florida with some friends, every rap concert, and also to Jamaica with my friend, Chell, her mom, and boyfriend at the time. I was living the life; drinking, smoking, and partying.

I started dating another guy who was also in the streets. Now this guy, Delsin, was different from everyone I met. I met him through my best friend, Shawnell. He was really down to earth and was the first guy that actually spoke life into me. Daily, he expressed how precious I was, commented on how hard I worked, told me that I was strong and deserved someone who would give me the world. He was like an angel that God placed in my life. He would make sure that I got to work every day, fed me when I got off or brought me something to eat and we stayed together every night. At this time, I did not have my own place because I gave it up since my plan was to go to the Marines. Delsin, however, ensured we stayed together every night. His dad had moved back with his wife so we would stay between his dad's apartment, Tonya's, and hotels. There would be many nights he would be running around making money and I would wake up and

84

we would be at a hotel. No matter what the case was, he made sure he stayed with me every night. Things moved fast and we bonded quickly. What I wanted and whatever he thought I wanted or needed he provided. He truly treated me like a queen. He made sure I had the best weed and something rolled every time I got off work. As we would sit across from each other and eat dinner, he always made me take my glasses off and looked into my hazel eyes and told me how beautiful I was and how much he adored me. We had some great times. Everything we did brought peace, lots of smiles, and joy. I continued to work, but I did not have to work overtime because he made sure I was cool. He took me to meet his mom and to an indoor water park not too far from his mom's house. His mom and stepdad welcomed me into their home and were beyond nice to me. That was a weekend I will always remember. The time we had was so peaceful and fun. Peace actually consumed me while in his presence.

One day he told me that he had some running around to do and since I did not have to work, I went over to Tonya's house. I was there chilling and decided to call him to check on him since we did not go too long without talking to one another. Some woman answered his phone and then hung up. My heart dropped. He called me shortly after and heard the hurt in my voice. He automatically asked me where I was so he could be on his way there. As I waited, I cried, thinking, "This dude ain't no good." On the other hand, I felt like what I was feeling could not be true because all he had been doing and showing me did not add up to him messing with another woman. He showed up at my sister's house with this huge bouquet of red roses and looked me in my face and said he was sincerely sorry. He had gone over the girl's house and allowed her to use his car. He left his phone in his car and she answered it when it rang. He said that he had not been messing with her since he had been with me and I should know that because we stayed together every night. He promised that would never happen again and everything in me believed him. Everything he had shown and done for me up until that point superseded that girl answering his phone.

After kicking it with him for a few months straight he called me while I was at work and he did not sound right. He said that he needed to talk to me when I got off. After work, I got a ride to Tonya's and he met me there. When he arrived, he didn't appear to be himself and his mood was totally off. He looked me in my face with so much pain in his eyes. He said that he was about to have to do nine months in the halfway house and that he had a lot going on. He said that he really did not feel that we were at the point where he could trust me with his cars and things and the woman before me would hold him down. He stated that he had been going strong with me and had not messed with her the entire time we were rocking, but he could not find it in himself to lie to me about the situation and end up hurting me by dealing with her while he was away. Again, I was left in shock. How the fuck do we go all this time, staying with each other every night, in each other's presence daily, and you have not grown to trust me? He said that he could have just lied and dealt with both of us while he was away, but I did not deserve to be lied to and hurt. Sadly, saying what he said still hurt me. I did not look at the situation as if he was not trying to hurt me. I looked at it as if he was putting another broad before me. As he left my sister's house, I ran after him, begging him to trust me and to not leave me. I begged him. Running after him gave me flash backs of when I ran after my mom in the rain, begging her not to leave.

So there I was again, stuck with pain to endure. During this time, Aaron was chasing after me, but I was refusing to give him the time of day. I did not entertain him at all when he would call my phone, trying to apologize and come see me. He showed up at Tonya's house, yelling my name and calling the house phone, three or four in the morning, because he was unaware that I no longer lived there. Tonya would call me, yelling at me about his behaviors. No matter how many times she told him that I did not live there, he continued to pop up. At this time, I was not dealing with Aaron and in shock about what Delsin said to me. Therefore, my anger, drinking, and smoking were at an all-time high.

One night, I was in my same routine of working 3 pm-11 pm and getting off work and going to the local neighborhood bar. Aaron called me numerous times, so I finally gave in and answered. I was super pissed at Delsin, so that is what really made me answer. He begged me to hook up with him and I refused. I talked so badly to him about him bringing that girl to my house and saying that he loved me when he did not. During that conversation he insisted that he loved me and said sorry so many times. I would follow up with, "I am not fucking with you ever again because you did me dirty." He never got upset or raised his voice which was unusual, given the way I was communicating with him. That night he called me for about two hours trying to get me to meet up with him. He stated that he did not want to have sex, he wanted to take me out and to see me. I joked with him and stated that the only way that would happen is if he got me the Jordan's that were dropping the next morning. He promised he would get them for me if I would just tell him where I was. I then told him he would have to not only get me a pair but also his daughter because he couldn't buy a woman some shoes and not his child. He laughed and I told him I would call him back shortly. I continued to drink until I blacked out and I never answered any of his additional calls. I woke up at Tonya's house the next morning, with all of these missed calls. I assumed the calls were about going to get the Jordan's that morning. I was initially pissed because it was around 11 am and I knew the Jordan's in my size would be sold out by the time I made it to the store. I had missed numerous calls from Aaron and other people. I saw that my best friend, Shawnell had called me, so I called her back first. The sound in her voice was frightening. She yelled, "Genafie, did you hear what happened last night?" I responded, "No, I was drunk as hell and blacked out at Tonya's house." She went on to say, "Aaron got killed last night." I started yelling at the top of my lungs. I told her that there was no way and that I had just spoken with him the previous night. She stated that he was killed around 1:30 am. The last missed call I received from him was a little after 1 am. At that moment so much guilt consumed my heart. Our last conversation consisted of me talking reckless to him and all I recall was him keeping his cool and begging for me to tell him where I was. Guilt took me over because if I had only told him where I was, maybe he would not have been in that bar and got killed. I also later thought that maybe God spared my life a third time because

I could have been killed or witnessed his tragic death if I had met up with him at the bar.

How the fuck did I go from Delsin basically putting another woman before me, to Aaron dying? How was I to cope with those two things on top of all of the childhood trauma that had never been addressed? Like how was I to continue to cope? Like how? From the age of five, until I was 21, I had become accustomed to people leaving me. A healthy bond and attachment with my parents never existed and the two guys that did mean something to me had left me. Aaron would leave me forever, though.

I got an apartment, worked, drank, and smoked weed daily for approximately a year. During this time, I met Shawnell's cousin, Dana, and began dating him. I was 21, he was 35 and from the beginning, the relationship was unhealthy. What attracted me to him was the fact that he had custody of his two-year-old daughter. Something made me fall for all of his bullshit because of the love I had for her. This would be another unhealthy relationship I would indulge in.

CHAPTER 8

My Life Savers

Tonya remained a huge support. The local bar was up the street from her house, so there were many nights that I would go to her house and stay over, as opposed to going home. After a year of being intoxicated, she looked me in my eyes and said that I needed to get my shit together. She said, "All you do is drink and smoke and you are not a bar bitch. Get back into school and get your shit together. You had hopes and dreams to open a group home to help teenaged foster girls and being in the bar every day is not it. Genafie, get your shit together. Go back to community college and register for classes like today. The shit you are doing is not going to cut it." She also became aware of me dating Dana. She knew him because they had grown up together and she felt he was too old for me, but she did not judge my decision.

After the conversation with Tonya, I went back to

school and registered for both summer terms. I then completed the following fall, spring, and summer terms that following summer in order to have enough credits to apply for a four-year school. I would begin to see a commercial promoting a church and the pastor was so inspirational. I started going to that church and the pastor was amazing. I was still smoking weed and drinking, but slowed down somewhat. I started to attend church regularly because it seemed like I felt better every time I left. A form of peace that I had never experienced before would come over me from the time I walked into the sanctuary, until the time I left. Although I continued to smoke weed, I would remember what was preached during the sermons and I tried to apply it to my daily life.

Tonya also told me that she had seen Delsin and he had asked about me and wanted my number, but she would not give it to him. He gave his number to Tonya, but I never called. Right when I completed that spring term, at the age of 23, I spoke with my advisor and told her my career goals, which consisted of being a therapist, as well as opening a group home for teenaged foster girls. She suggested that I apply to the University of Pittsburgh School of Social Work program because it was one of the best programs in the nation. She also suggested that I apply to Carlow and Point

Park because they were local schools with a Social Work program. I needed 60 credits in order to get accepted into these schools. I applied to all three schools, then realized that I would only have 59 credits once I completed both summer terms. I then became completely discouraged. All of the programs started in the fall, but I would have to take a one credit course during the time that I wanted to start the 4 year school and then wait until the following fall to get into the program. I was so upset at the thought of having to wait a whole year because of one credit.

Shortly after applying to the four year universities, I found out that I was pregnant by Dana. I had been dealing with him off and on for a little over two years. During our break-ups, on a few occasions, I dealt with other guys but those encounters did not last long. I would automatically drop them once they did anything that I was not fond of. The main reason I continued to deal with him was his baby girl that lived with him. I did everything for her as if she was my child, but he would not allow me to ever fully bond with her. When I told him that I was pregnant, he wanted me to get an abortion because he did not want any more kids at that time. He also stated that I was ruining my life by having a baby. He promised me that I would not graduate from college if I kept the baby. So, I made a vow to not only prove him wrong, but to get my degree for the sake of the child I was about to bring into this world. Finding out that I was pregnant brought me pure joy. I felt like my baby would be someone who would finally love me unconditionally and someone who would never leave me. I promised myself that I would protect her and give her the world. Tonya continued to tell me that she had seen Delsin and that he would always ask about me. One day, she told me that she had been seeing him with her friend's daughter, but I brushed it off like I did not care. Even though he continued to ask about me, what really prevented me from making contact with him was knowing that he was messing with someone.

I received my acceptance letter from Carlow and they accepted me with the 59 credits. I was excited and immediately scheduled a tour. I attended by myself and the admission's director asked if my parents wished to partake in this process and I would sadly state, "No." She then stated that I would need my parents' income information to apply for financial aid and I then embarrassingly explained that I was a ward of the court and aged out of CYF care and the school would use my income, not my parents. Upon completion of the tour I was not too fond of the school, plus it was awfully expensive and I would only attend if Pitt did not accept me. I then received my acceptance letter from Pitt and yelled so loudly!!! So much joy filled my heart. I then realized that the letter stated that the acceptance was only official if I had the 60 credits and of course, I only had 59. I called the school and was informed that the school would accept me with 59 credits. I would have to pass my summer courses, to have 59 credits and I did everything needed to successfully pass. I called Tonya and shared that joyful moment with her. She automatically told me I had to graduate because I was bringing a baby into this world, so that was a top priority. I completed that summer course on August 7 and started as a junior at Pitt on August 23. I thought I was on top of the world walking on that campus.

My experience at Pitt brought so much to light about how I functioned. As I sat in lectures, I totally felt that the professors were talking directly to me when discussing trauma, addiction, and mental illness. Discussing topics around generational addiction, mental health issues, poverty, teen pregnancy; they all hit home. The more risk one faces, the more likely they are to face negative outcomes later in life. I became self-aware of how one's childhood had a major effect on how one functioned as a parent and when they became an adult. I learned methods to counteract the negative outcomes I was at a high percentage to encounter. I can honestly say that I was extremely shell shocked when I walked into my first class because I had only seen about two other blacks in a class of over a hundred students. The staff and faculty in the social work program were very culturally sensitive, non-judgmental, helpful, uplifting, and encouraging. Pitt taught me how I was to conduct myself in a professional manner and how to push and work hard for my dreams and desires.

At around five months pregnant, I took my car to be detailed because it was filthy, and I would feel someone come behind me and wrap their arms around me. As I heard his voice, I realized it was Delsin. When I turned around, he smiled at me, but I also saw pain in his eyes. As he smiled, he said, "Yo, you are pregnant." I smiled and responded, "Yes." He grabbed my stomach and said that should have been my baby and shook his head. He took my number and said he would be calling me. He also told me not to worry about paying for the detail because he would pay for it.

Around this time, I was aware that he was messing with someone, but he came around as a listening ear and gave me words of encouragement. He was so happy that I was attending Pitt and had no doubt that I would graduate. From the time I found out I was pregnant, I did not deal with the father of my child. He financially helped with everything I needed for her, but mentally and emotionally he was not there for me. He did not attend any of the pre-natal appointments with me. Delsin, on the other hand, continued to support me in any way that he could. He would continuously tell me how amazing, beautiful, and strong I was. He would tell me how intelligent I was and how I would be graduating from one of the best schools. He would come to my house during my pregnancy and bring me things to eat, and encourage and uplift me. He was like my peace through the storm. During this time, he didn't try to have sex with me. It was a friendship that I would never forget. I began to really love this guy because he was in my corner during a very critical time and he encouraged me more than anyone.

I did not know how to be a mom but I knew there were things I needed to work on, like patience. I wanted to have patience to be able to properly comfort and nurture my daughter. I needed to get rid of the anger inside of me because I would snap at the drop of a dime. I would not be able to smoke weed and drink anymore as a means to cope because I refused for my child to see me addicted to any drug. Additionally, the patterns of unhealthy relationships and risky behaviors stopped. I needed to take my spiritual walk more seriously, because that was the only thing that seemed to give me peace. With that in mind, I got baptized when I was five months pregnant and from that point on, it was like God immediately wiped all the pain away. I received peace that I had never felt before. I did not worry. I got up every day, happy and free from depression. I coped by reading my bible. The urge to smoke weed was automatically removed. I asked God to remove the anger in my heart and the foul language and he did. I asked him to show me how to be a mom. I wanted to be a mom like the white ladies on the TV shows. Taking their children to the park, reading to them daily, ensuring that they go to a good school, being calm and meek, not raising their voice, and being loving and nurturing. God blessed me with every one of those characteristics in my heart. Pregnant and all, I promised myself that I would graduate from Pitt, but it was very challenging. I attended the writing center, study groups, and made several friends who

would help me pass my courses.

Shawnell threw me a little baby shower. My mom, cousins, grandma, and aunts attended. My daughter's paternal grandmother also attended. My mom was her usual self, looking sad and not at all happy that she was about to be a grandmother. She and Shawnell thought it was ok to go into my car and smoke weed during the baby shower. I became beyond pissed at my best friend for even thinking that it was ok to smoke with my mom, because I would never disrespect her mom that way. I was equally annoyed that my mom thought it was cool to smoke weed with my friend. Lastly, why smoke weed in my car when I have to get in there after the baby shower? My mom ended up getting mad at me and leaving the baby shower. At this point, it was like every enjoyable moment was spoiled by someone. It seemed that nothing could be a joyous occasion when it came to celebrating anything pertaining to me. However, between the baby shower, my daughter's father, and Tonya, I was well prepared for the arrival of my daughter. She had over a year's worth of clothing and enough diapers to last at least six months.

A week past my due date, I was ready to have my baby. Tonya had work and wanted me to babysit for her. As an attempt to go into labor, I walked to her house which was about a mile from where I lived. I walked up and down her steps numerous times while I was at her house. When she got off at 11 pm, she took me home and shortly after I got home, I started to have contractions. I was able to take the contractions until about 3:30 am and around that time they became unbearable. Tonya came and picked me up and I had my baby girl at 11:48 am that morning.

Tonya was in the delivery room with me. She walked me through the entire delivery. Tonya would be the first person my daughter set eyes on. She did not initially cry when she came out and I became frantic, but Tonya promised me that she was fine. It turned out that that would be her temperament, because she would rarely cry as a baby or as a toddler. I named her Genafie LaShawn Brown. My "Tink Girl," is what I would call her. My grandma and Aunt May came to the hospital to see me when I had the baby. My grandma was mesmerized by her. My mom on the other hand, never showed.

I took a three month maternity leave from work and two weeks off from school. My professors were so surprised to see me back in class but they had no idea how hard I fought to get to this point and I was not going to mess it up. My first day back to class, Tonya kept my daughter. I cried the entire way to class and took several breaks to go into the bathroom to call Tonya and cry. She reassured me that my baby was safe and sent me pics of her during that entire three hour seminar. She could not enroll into day care until she was three months old, so in order for me to attend class Tonya, her dad, and his mom would keep her. Besides going to class, my baby was with me at all times. I breastfed her, took her on walks, sang, and read to her daily. She was such a calm and sweet baby. The look she gave me every morning brought me so much joy. Her dad not being around bothered me and I would have moments when I would express that to him, but that pushed me to be a better mom. I promised my baby girl that she would not endure anything that I did. I continued to develop a strong walk with Christ. I made sure she attended the best daycares and that she had the best life that I could provide.

I really did not look at her dad the same after he did not support me emotionally while I was pregnant, but I respected him because he made sure that I got everything I wanted and needed for her before and after she was born. A week after I had her, he would come see her and gave me some roses and a teddy bear. He uncovered her, looked at her and stated, "She's got my features." She was born with the exact nose as him and his mother. He then signed the birth certificate. We would communicate when it came to our daughter. His only request was for me not to sue him and at the time, there was no problem with him helping to take care of her, so I told him that I would agree to his request.

Delsin remained in my life, on a friendship level. I grew to have so much respect for him because, during my pregnancy, he never tried to sexually pursue me, but was a down to earth friend. I stopped having sex with my daughter's father once I found out that I was pregnant, and he wanted me to get an abortion. I then remained celibate until my daughter was 10 months. Delsin was the first guy that I actually dealt with after dropping them and that was only because he remained a huge support and comforted me during and after my pregnancy. Moreover, he always called and encouraged me to continue to go hard and do what was necessary to graduate from college. He did whatever it took for me and my daughter to be cool so I could graduate. Him doing that meant a lot to me. He also loved my daughter. She was not his child, but he loved her unconditionally. He would come to my house quite frequently and play with my daughter for hours and this melted my heart. At the time, I was not having sex with him and he loved us like no other. All he would ask me to do was cook for him and whenever he asked, I stopped what I was doing and cooked for him. From the time he saw me five months pregnant up until two months before my daughter turned one, Delsin and I refrained from any form of sexual relationship. I had not been with anyone for about a year and a half and he came to my house one day and one thing led to another. He remained a huge support for me and Tink. Although he was seeing someone, I looked at him as a friend and his support of me and my daughter superseded him dating another woman. Moreover, I felt that I trusted him and by this point I grew to love him on a much higher level. He brought me so much peace and happiness. Plus, why mess with anyone else when my main focus was on parenting my daughter and school, not a relationship. Moreover, he took great care of me and my daughter; we did not need or want for anything. Therefore, I looked at him as a friend and someone I could call when I wanted to be intimate.

My senior year of college consisted of me taking a couple classes and completing an internship. I ended up completing my internship at CYF. I knew one day I wanted to operate a group home for teenaged girls involved in CYF, so I was adamant about getting an internship there. Moreover, it would be a paid internship. Upon applying and getting accepted for the position, the field advisor informed me that I would not be able to intern there. Per the university policy, students could not complete an internship at an agency from which they received services. This time would be the first time I advocated for myself. I spoke with some higher ups at the University and was informed that if CYF permitted me, then I could intern there. I contacted the personnel at CYF and they agreed to make an exception for me. I learned so much at Pitt and at my internship and I implemented what I was taught in my role as a mother. I remained sober as I breastfed Genafie, until she was one and would continue to develop a stronger relationship with God. Tonya and Genafie were my lifesavers. Because of those two, my daily walk and purpose in life changed. Tonya could have twenty dollars and if I needed fifteen, she would give it to me. No one had ever treated me like Tonya did. Moreover, no man ever treated me like Delsin. He treated me like I was the most precious and beautiful woman who walked the earth. His role in my life was so important. From the time I became pregnant with Tink, up until that point, he too was a huge support and one of my lifesavers.

My baby girl's 1st birthday came around so fast. She slept the entire party. The space I was in around this time was a joyous place. I loved everything about my daughter and made sure that she had a life way better than the one I had growing up. She enjoyed listening to my voice, as I would sing her lullabies or read her books as she sat on my lap. When she turned one, she had her own little library of books. Her dad remained involved financially, but really did not see her often. He would attempt to sleep with me, but failed to build a bond with our daughter and that turned me off. He did go above and beyond to help with her first birthday celebration and he was present. We remained cordial but were not intimate. Delsin, at this time, was around me and little Genafie often and had built a bond with her. He was not going to miss her first birthday so he too attended. It appeared that her dad was not too fond of that and although Tonya liked Delsin, she mentioned something to me about him showing up. I was somewhat uncomfortable, but at the same time, he was there for me emotionally and mentally and I had a high level of love and respect for him.

Chell was in the Marines and placed in Hawaii so a week after Genafie's 1st birthday we would go to Hawaii to visit. On my stroll through the airport I would meet and take pictures with James Harrison. He too was on his way to Hawaii to play in the Pro-Bowel. While in Hawaii Chell and I fell out over something beyond stupid. On the other hand for the most part I enjoyed the beautiful scenery beaches, the zoo, clubs, and Pro-Bowel.

I graduated a few months after Genafie's first birthday. I ended up graduating from Pitt with a 3.2 GPA. I would have had a higher GPA, but I never had the full opportunity to just focus on school. I continued to work, attend school full-time, and was a single mom. Again, my mom would not be present for my graduation. My sister Rhonda and Tonya were there though. Delsin did not attend my graduation because he was in the streets heavy around this time, but him helping to pay my tuition made me happy. Tonya held my baby girl as I walked across the stage and received my degree. As I sat at graduation and thought about having accomplished something that was so extravagant, I felt empty. I sat there pondering why neither one of my parents would be present to witness this great achievement.

I automatically had a job post-graduation because my

internship was a paid placement and I was obligated to work for the agency for a year. I loved working at CYF. I enjoyed the families and the children that I served. Helping people get their kids back is what I loved most. Removing people's children was probably as traumatic for me as it was for the families. I felt really empowered and worked with families in a capacity so the children could remain in their home. I would continue to grow professionally and remain at this job for many years, but my role as a mother was my main priority.

CHAPTER 9

A Degree Did Not Change the Attraction

My first-year post undergrad was good. I continued to grow professional and I loved my job. I really loved that I worked Monday through Friday, had great benefits, and could take off whenever I needed to. However, I did not like the fact that I would have to work late most evenings. After changing Genafie's daycare center a few times, she was finally enrolled at a touch notch facility. The first daycare center was located in a home residence. It was reasonably priced and the owner seemed nice. However, Genafie came home a few times with bite marks on her and the owner could not tell me what happened. One day, I arrived to pick Genafie up and observed another toddler trying to pick her up out of her car seat. Around this time, a local home childcare center was shut down because another child picked up a baby, dropped the baby, resulting in the baby dying. Observing that resulted in me quickly removing Genafie from that center. She was removed from the second center because she came home with bleach all over her shirt and the staff could not tell me what had occurred. I then looked at about ten daycares in the neighborhood in which we resided, but did not get a good feeling from any of them. Therefore, I began to search for daycares in the closest suburban neighborhood and located one. Because of the location, it was very expensive, but I felt comfortable dropping her off there every morning and felt that she was in safe hands while I worked. Due to my long days at work I would drop her off at 7:30 am and pick her up at 6 pm, when the center closed. On many days I would be leaving court or a client's home and fly through traffic to get to the daycare center on time to pick her up.

Genafie was my pride and joy and I would never allow her to stay the night over anyone's house, which resulted in me doing very little outside of work. If Delsin wanted to take me out anywhere, Tonya or my friend, Kathy, would babysit for me. Kathy and I stopped hanging as much when I got pregnant with Genafie because I had stopped smoking weed. However, now, I talked to her often and although she was way older than I was, we regarded each other as family.

One day, I permitted Genafie to go to my little sister's house because my mom was there and she wanted to see her.

They had taken Genafie to the park and when I came to pick her up, she was dirty, especially her feet and I went off. My mom and sister looked at me like I was crazy and said that I was overreacting. They said that she was at the park playing and her feet got dirty because she had on sandals. I never allowed my baby girl to be dirty and my actions that day showed that. Most times, to eliminate needing a babysitter, I would do lunch dates with Delsin because my office location was located near a lot of restaurants. My role as a mother brought me so much joy.

I kept my same routine, which was: work, pick Genafie up, and cook for Delsin, when he would call or show up at my house. Anytime he wanted me to cook, hook up or go out, I did. He did anything for me, so in return, I did what he asked. The first time Genafie stayed the night elsewhere, was when she was about eighteen months and Delsin wanted me to go out of town with him. My Aunt Kathy babysat Genafie for me and although Kathy would allow no harm to come to Genafie, I was anxious the entire trip. I missed her like crazy and worried the entire time. Delsin gave Kathy a hundred dollars a day to keep her. You would have thought I packed enough clothes, food, and diapers for a month just looking at the amount of stuff I took to my aunt's. My entire time away, I blew my aunt's phone up, but she would let me hear her voice and assured me that Genafie was fine. While away with Delsin, he would see me break down for the first time. At this time, he was dating me and another woman and I wanted that to end. The last night of our trip, I stated that I did not wish for him to do that anymore. I told him I wanted him to leave the girl alone and just be with me and my daughter. One thing about him was that he was always open and honest with me.

Our friendship was deep and on a level that many relationships never develop. He was a best friend that I had become intimate with. He was not aware of my childhood trauma, because at this time I had never expressed it to anyone. I was embarrassed by the trauma; therefore it became a secret I kept to myself. In the six years of knowing him, all he saw me do was smile. He had only seen me cry once and when he said he was not going to do what I asked, I broke down and cried myself to sleep. Deep down inside, he was another individual I felt that let me down. My love and respect for him did not diminish, but how I viewed him did. His decision made me feel like he put someone before me, just like my mom, dad, and every other man I had dealt with up to this point. I loved him so much and did decide to continue to deal with him, but I also felt like I really was not enough. I felt like no one would ever fully love me and put me first.

My love for him made me play tricks with my own mind.

I minimized what he was doing and just looked at him as my best friend, but also someone I was intimate with. My family all knew that I was dating him, but I never stated that he was my boyfriend. I did not identify what we had going on as being unhealthy because around this time no woman came to me about him. We never argued, nor did he ever raise his voice or put his hands on me.

My life continued to consist of being a mother, work, and holding Delsin down when he called. A month before Genafie's second birthday, he went to jail, but posted a $250,000 bond and was able to get out. I did not know the seriousness of the case, but he did tell me that he would have to do jail time because he got caught with a lot of drugs. When that situation occurred, it seemed like something about him changed. He started to become more distant from me. A few months passed and one night we hooked up and went out and when I woke up, he was not there. He would never leave without waking me up, giving me a kiss, and telling me he loved me before he left. Something was just off about him. I did not talk to him for a few days and then got a call from him. He was in jail and stated that the feds had picked him up and he was at the local county jail. He stated that when he was recently arrested the feds were involved, but they allowed him to post bond as a method to continue to watch him. At the time, he did not know what would happen, but would keep me updated.

Time went by, we would talk on the phone but things were not looking good for him. The feds were trying to give him 25 years. After going to court, he finally took a plea of 15 years. When I got the call, the news broke my heart. Like something left me when he said he got 15 years. That call took me to a place that I wish I never went back to. I started smoking weed again. I would never smoke around my daughter but when I got off of work and put her to bed, in order to ease my mind, I would smoke, in an attempt to be taken away from the hurt and painful thoughts. I would drink here and there but not like I used to.

I missed him, so visiting him would bring me joy. One day I went out and I took Genafie to my little sister's house, because my mom was visiting and wanted to see her. As I left, my mom and sister joked about the last time she was there, when her feet were dirty. They laughed as they stated that they would be sure she would be clean when I came to pick her up. I picked her up that night and we went home. I woke up the next morning, forgetting that I had picked her up and got on the road to go visit Delsin. About 35 minutes out, I called my mom to see what Tink was doing and she stated she was not there. She stated that I had picked her up the night before.

I was adamant that I had not picked her up. I was thinking that she was joking so I called my sister. She too stated that Tink was not there. Again, I thought they were joking. Once they expressed adamantly that she was not there I snapped and started, "Where the fuck is my daughter?" My heart dropped and it felt like a part of me lost it. Tears streamed down my face as I drove. I got off the next exit and did hundred miles per hour back to Pittsburgh. I called my one sister on my dad's side because she was a police officer and I informed her of what was going on. She asked for my sister's address and the police automatically went to my little sister's house. I called her dad and he also went to my little sister's house. After doing all of that, I looked back at Tink's car seat crying and something clicked. I recalled picking her up and putting her in her bed when we got home last night. I automatically panicked and rushed back to my house. I got there so fast. When I went into my house, I ran to Tink's room. Her bedroom was right across from mine. It appeared that she had just awakened and was climbing onto my bed, something she did every morning. I picked her up and cried with her in my arms and promised I would never do anything like that again. I called my sister, the police officer, and told her that I had Tink. I was directed to bring Tink to my little sister's house to show the police that I had her and I did just

113

that. Although her dad was not present much, when I pulled up, he was pissed. Police dogs were everywhere and my mom was at the headquarters being questioned. Several of my sisters were there and they were all crying and pissed.

At that very moment, I questioned myself. How was I even in this situation with Delsin? Running to a jail to visit a guy had landed me here. Like, how did I fall in love with a guy that was dealing mega drugs? With someone who was dealing with me and another woman? Moreover, what made me settle for that? How did I fall into this trap, like how? Why was I attracted to a drug dealer, when I had a great career and everything going for myself? I graduated from one of the best universities and had a good job, but I remained attracted to street guys. Why? How? What the hell, Genafie?

That would be the last time that I would get on the road to visit him, but the communication continued. When he went away, I found myself looking for a man that could take his role. I was still attracted to street guys. Finding someone to fill his shoes was a very difficult task. The lack of his presence had a huge effect on me. For the previous three years, he had been my number one fan, encourager, and he also spoiled the hell out of me. I engaged in several non-meaningful relationships, trying to fill his void, which left me empty. No one was ever allowed around my daughter and no one could equal up to a quarter of what Delsin brought to the table. He was my protector, provider, confidante, and was the one person who brought me peace. We had a very open relationship and I told him how I felt and what I was doing. I never lied or kept anything from him, as honesty was something that we expected from each other. Our calls were always so purposeful. He would always continue to encourage me to be strong, work hard, and be a good mom. He always expressed his love for me and told me how beautiful I was. He always asked about Tink and expressed how much he missed her. He understood my reasoning for not coming up to visit anymore, but would share how much he wanted to see me. For the first three years that he was away, I maintained full contact with him until I found someone who I thought could fill his shoes.

CHAPTER 10

Can I Get a Break

One day, I returned home to receive a letter. The letter was not from Delsin, but from Mercer County Child Protective Services. The letter stated that a relative of mine was in foster care and the agency wanted to know if I would be a caregiver for him. I immediately called because six months prior, my brother, Lavar had completed a paternity test for a child that was prospectively his. The child's mother was in jail and she was married, therefore in the state of Pennsylvania the husband is automatically, legally assigned to be the child's father. However, there was no way the husband could be the child's father because he was incarcerated when the girl got pregnant and had remained incarcerated. Therefore, Lavar completed a DNA test and the child turned out to be his child. Child Protective Services tried to allow my brother to care for the baby but the agency did not feel he was appropriate to do so, therefore my nephew was put in foster care. I recalled being in foster care and none of my family taking me in, so I said that I would care for him, not knowing how difficult it would be. He had been in four different placements prior to moving with me and he was only nine months.

Taking care of my nephew, Jaziah (Jay), really became a huge chore. All he did was cry. He would scream at the top of his lungs all day, every day. I felt extremely bad for the day care staff. Getting a babysitter was always a no go. No one wanted to babysit him because of his very difficult temperament. The only free time I had was while he was at daycare. I would try my best to do everything needed during daycare hours. He was also quite developmentally delayed. He did not walk until he was almost 16 months, so I was left to carry a heavy baby around all the time. I had three different therapists coming to my home to work with him. I went from having a very calm child, with an easy temperament, to the total opposite. Getting sleep was very difficult for about the first year and a half that he was with me. He just refused to sleep through the night. He would wake up crying very loudly, several times throughout the night. Comforting him was not feasible. A bottle, rocking him, walking around with him, nor holding him soothed him. He would just scream. Many times just to get some sleep I would put him in his crib, shut the bedroom door and ignore him until I fell back to sleep. Eventually he would stop crying. I found myself doing that often, as his squealing screams were unbearable at times. Going out in public or to someone's house was extremely embarrassing because he would scream the entire time. I left many parties, gatherings, and grocery stores due to so many people staring at me because of his screaming. After he had been placed with me for approximately six months, the courts gave me primary custody and guardianship over him; therefore, CPS was no longer involved with him. Due to his young age, they wanted me to adopt him but I decided not to do that. His mother had to serve at least three years. She said that when she got out she would stay clean and get herself together, so I wanted to keep the door open for her, or my brother, to be able to petition the court for custody if they wished to do so in the future.

My relationship with Christ was not as strong as it was when I first got saved and gave birth to Tink. However, I continued to attend church at least twice a week, Sunday service and bible study. I would always hope that Jay would fall asleep on our way to church so I would be able to hear the service. Sometimes I was lucky; other days he would have a fit. It got to the point where I considered calling CPS and asking for them to come get him. While at church one day, one of the ministers saw me crying and asked what was wrong. I told her about the difficulty that I was having caring for him and that I was considering giving him back to CPS. She laid hands on him and prayed over me. That prayer worked because he became less difficult to care for. He would have his moments, but not to the point when he initially came with me. There were times when things would get difficult and I would immediately have one of the ministers lay hands on him and that seemed to work.

One day, as I was getting ready for work, I noticed a lump in my leg. It did not hurt or bother me. I told Tonya and she said to schedule an appointment with a primary care physician. I did not have one at the time, because I hadn't seen a doctor in many years. The last time I recalled being seen by a primary care physician was when I was placed in a group home and that was when I was fourteen. Tonya gave me her doctor's number and I called and got an appointment within the next few weeks. She completed a full exam and stated that I appeared well. She stated that the lump was most likely a cyst, but recommended that I get blood work done. I left that office and immediately got my blood work completed. The physician called me a few days later expressing high concern about my blood work, specifically my white and red blood cells and liver enzyme levels. She recommended that I be seen by a hematologist. I made an appointment with one and additional blood work was completed. I was checked for everything in the book and nothing was found. I was then required to complete a bone marrow biopsy and that was the worst experience of my life. The doctor took a needle and put it into my spine, right at the bottom of my back, above my butt. The area was not numb and I was informed that it would not be too painful but that was a huge lie. I screamed at the top of my lungs. I would get a call a week later to inform me that they did not get an adequate sample and I would need to go through the process a second time and I would do so. I had so much flexibility and benefit time from my job that the medical appointments did not interfere with my job. I attended a follow up appointment and was informed that there was nothing wrong with my blood, as it was producing normally. However, I was told that something with my liver may be causing my blood work to be off. It was then recommended that I be seen by a Hepatologist.

I would undergo more and more blood work, and nothing was found. I then had to complete a liver biopsy because the Hepatologist stated that he thought I had an autoimmune disorder, but a liver biopsy would be the only way he would be able to make a diagnosis. I completed the biopsy and was informed that I had a disorder called auto-immune hepatitis. I immediately went off because I was ignorant of the disorder and when he mentioned hepatitis, I thought the worst. He explained that hepatitis meant liver damage. He said that the auto-immune portion means that your immune system is working against its own body. Therefore, the auto-immune disorder caused me to have liver damage. He said that I did not get it from anyone, nor could I spread it. There were not a lot of studies on the disorder and it could only be treated through medication. He said that there was no way of knowing what caused the disorder, but that the body just starts working against itself. He reported only treating four people in which the disorder went into remission. Most people he treated with this disorder remained on medication for the rest of their lives. I looked the doctor in his face and stated that I would be the fifth patient, because God was going to heal me. His response was, "I can't say that to you." I then started on steroids and other immune system suppressant medications. The steroids caused me to gain weight, develop anxiety, become easily agitated and experience insomnia. When I told this to the doctor, he suggested another medication to offset the side effects. On numerous occasions I would get calls from his nurse telling me he ordered my meds to be changed without explaining the rationale behind the changes. I ended up becoming frustrated with that doctor and got transferred to another practice. I found myself wondering what the hell I did to deserve this. It was like my life only consisted of bad things. I was tired of dating guys who were not worth my while, nor on my level. I was tired of life and all of the obstacles I continued to face. I was extremely tired of everything.

My baby girl was beginning kindergarten shortly after I got diagnosed. We lived in a predominantly white neighborhood. The area was known for being racist and I did not want my child attending school in that district so I enrolled her at a Charter school. Her dad continued to come around infrequently but would help whenever needed. His lack of involvement did bother me, but I tried not to allow it to cause me to be upset. My baby girl was so intelligent. She was reading at four years old and her test scores were off the charts for kindergarten and first grade. The school curriculum did not appear to be challenging for her so I transferred her to a private school by second grade.

Church attendance remained a priority and I gained a lot of knowledge because the pastor was amazing. After hearing a sermon, I wrote a list of what I wanted in a man. The list was very specific, from his career, to his height and anything you can think of in between. One thing I did not want was someone in the streets selling drugs. I promised myself I would not deal with anyone else living that type of life because it would not get me anywhere. I wrote that letter and about a year later I would run into a man who would have almost everything I wrote on the list. Moreover, I felt that he could fill Delsin's shoes.

I met him as I pumped my gas at the local gas station. Nate got out of his Benz and walked into the gas station. When he came out, he came over and politely asked me my name. He was attractive and did not present himself like most guys. We exchanged numbers and went on our way. We would begin dating and hit it off fast. We talked and were together daily. He worked for the City and I worked for the County. We both had good jobs that we had been at for years, as well as great benefits. He had two kids and so did I. Things looked very good for us. The only thing about him was that he was living with his parents and had two baby's mothers. Those were two things on my list that did not add up to what I wanted in a man, but I compromised because he was good to me and my kids.

Additionally, I grew to trust his parents and felt that they were some amazing and supportive people. One thing I wrote on my list was for my man's parents to be caring and treat my daughter and nephew like their own and his parents did just that. Around this time, I rarely allowed my daughter and nephew to go anywhere and his parents stepping up and babysitting helped me get the free time I needed so that Nate and I could go out, which we often did. Things were really moving quickly. I met him in January and kept saying to him, "We'll see how things go when summertime hits." Well when summertime hit, he stayed out all night once, but said that he was drunk and fell asleep over his friend's house. He had never done that before, so I believed him. The first year of us dating, we took several vacations alone, as well as ones with the kids. I tried to get him to move in with me, but he refused, stating that he was not ready to do that. My attraction to Nate continued to grow the more I observed the kind of father he was. His son had sickle cell anemia and he would make sure that he went to all of his required medical appointments, completed any necessary blood work, and during his hospital stays, he remained at his son's bedside.

Being a mother remained my top priority. Genafie loved to run so I signed her up for the track team that my foster mother's grandchildren ran for. I remembered having seen them run when I was young. They were some amazing track stars. They all had potential and would blow past all of their competitors. Genafie was the smallest and youngest runner, because she was only five, so she did not compete too well but in the track seasons to come, she became a beast. My nephew, Jaziah, was around three at the time and he continued to receive early intervention services. I made sure that all of his needs were always met.

I continued to have contact with Delsin for the first six months of dating Nate. After a while, I felt that it was time to have a difficult conversation with Delsin regarding my relationship. I told Delsin that I was dating someone and that I felt that Nate was the one. I shared that I felt like I was cheating on Nate by continuing to have contact with him. I informed him that we would no longer be able to communicate. He asked me how long I had been dating Nate and I told him that it had been six months. His response was, "You're going to tell me you can't talk to me after dating a nigga for six months? He's going to hurt you just like the other dudes did." He hung up on me and I did not talk to him again. A few weeks after that conversation, Nate put me on his cell phone family plan so my phone number was changed and Delsin had no means to call me if he wanted to. I did tell Nate about my relationship with Delsin when we first started dating, but implied that Delsin and I were only friends. After ending it with Delsin, I told Nate the truth about my relationship with him.

My landlord at the time had passed away and his

children inherited his property, so I had to move. My mom also needed to move, so in an attempt to try to build a relationship with her, I asked her if she wanted to find a house big enough for me, her, and the kids and she stated that she did. Nate and his brother helped us move into the home. The relationship building plan with my mom did not last long. She stayed with us for a few months and while she was there I got on my grind and worked at a travel agency, jitney station, and of course at my full time job, as a social worker. She would keep the kids for me when I worked. One day she called me and told me that Jay had jumped off of the dresser into the dresser drawer and that his nose was mangled. I rushed home to see that the right side of his nose had actually lifted off of his face. I took him to the emergency room and they numbed him and sewed his nose back onto his face. The doctors wanted me to help hold him down but I could not stomach the sight or the pain as he screamed out when they tried to work on him. They ended up putting him in what appeared to be a strait jacket. I was surprised that CPS was never called on me when it came to Jay. This was the second time he had needed stitches in a year. The first time, the daycare called me to tell me that he fell and hit his head off the window ledge, resulting in a laceration by his left eyebrow. He was always sick so taking him to be seen was routine.

The attempt to bond and grow a relationship with my mom went totally left. We weren't seeing eye to eye one day, resulting in us arguing. I left the house. When I returned, as I stood on the steps on my way to the second floor, I could hear her talking with my grandma. My mom was telling my grandma that I recently said that my cousin, on numerous occasions, attempted to sexually abuse me and my grandma's boyfriend had sexually abused another family member. Now I did tell my mom that as a means of opening up to her so she could be aware of some of the things I encountered growing up. My mom and grandma went on to say that I was lying and that the things I had said did not occur. I can honestly say that was the day that I disrespected my mother to a level I never did before. How the fuck can my mom and grandma say I was lying about something that I know happened? I would never call my child a liar if she told me that someone did something to her. My mom did not know I was listening until I tried to get into her bedroom and when I noticed the door was locked, I tried to break it down. I then ran out of the house crying and called Nate. I was in disbelief that my own mother and grandmother would say that I was lying about incidents that occurred more than once. This would be another situation when she would not take responsibility for the things that happened to her children while she was an addict. All she focused on was being disrespected, but failed to look at the reason that the disrespect was occurring in the first place. She moved out shortly after this incident and it would just be me and my two little ones again. This incident really made hate steam in my heart for her and my grandmother.

Since the passing of my dad, my sister Rhonda would always call me, trying to build a relationship with me and my daughter. With my busy life, most of the time she would not get me on the line, but instead she'd leave a voicemail. I would always hear the sincerity in her voice, which told me that her intentions were genuine. I wish I would have taken every opportunity she tried to build with me because she ended up getting ill and dying from bone marrow cancer. That was what our dad had also passed from. None of my other siblings ever tried to get to know me, but she did, and it was too late to build, because she was taken so fast. Prior to her passing, I went to go see her in the hospital because she really wanted to see me. This was her second time with bone marrow cancer. She looked very ill and lost a large amount of weight. I visited her daily and saw that she could barely breathe, but appeared to be putting up a fight. One day, before I left, she said she wanted to take a walk. We walked down the hall and she was so weak. When leaving, I had some hope, thinking that she would beat cancer again but ended up getting a call the very next morning saying that she had passed away. It hurt my heart when she died. Very few family members came to my college graduation, but she did. She knew the date of my graduation and just showed up. She looked for me but could not find me. She found me after seeing my daughter. She knew my daughter looked like me so when she saw her she went up to Tonya and asked if Tink was my daughter. She expressed how proud she was of me. My mom and dad were not there but my oldest sister was and I loved her for that. She did not have life insurance, but I had saved some money from working so hard, so I was able to pay for most of her funeral arrangements.

Around this time, my granddad passed away. He did not have coverage either and I would also help pay for a large portion of his funeral. One thing after another would happen and I had to face everything, day by day; go to work, be a parent, and remain in my right state of mind. Nate would be by my side through all of these storms.

CHAPTER II

Happily Ever After is What I Thought

Nate and I dated for a year and a half and were together daily. Although he said that he did not want to move in, he stayed at my house almost every day. During this year and a half, he did stay out all night, a few times, but said that it was due to him being drunk and passing out at his friend's. I had no reason not to trust him because, outside of work, we were like two peas in a pod. Moreover, we had the codes to each other's phones and I checked his phone often, but never found anything. I felt he was the one and he felt the same. I wanted him to move in with me, but we felt that we needed to be married first. One night, lying in bed together, I asked him his thoughts about getting married and he stated that he always wanted to get married and wanted to marry me. I suggested that we get married soon and then have a big wedding later and he agreed. A few weeks after that conversation, we got married at the church that I was attending. His parents and our four children were present. I did not have any fear in my heart. I was happy to say I was someone's wife.

Marriage was not always peaches and cream. Nate and his children moved in and at that time Nate's son and Tink started second grade at a private school. The workload and schoolwork were easy for Tink, but his son struggled. I would put in a lot of time and dedication to make sure he got all of his assignments completed correctly. We paid for reading programs and I would take him because I was determined for him to be able to read on the correct grade level. Cooking, cleaning, raising four kids, being a wife, and working full-time was much harder than I had imagined. Some days I would be extremely exhausted and would become easily frustrated with the kids. One thing that they were sure of was that I loved them because my actions showed them that. I would hug and kiss them every night and tell them that I loved them. Birthday parties and holidays seemed like they were occurring monthly. All of the kids celebrated the holidays with Nate and me. I never had a Christmas so I would go all out for them. They got video games, bikes, motorcycles, racetracks, baby dolls, doll houses, clothes, shoes, and an abundance of other toys. There was nothing they wanted for. I treated all four kids as if they were mine.

My rent at the time was nine hundred dollars and I felt like buying a home would be cheaper. My plan was to buy a home with cash so we did not have a mortgage and our largest bill would be the kids' school tuition. Nate suggested that we move with his parents for a while, save up money, and buy a house with cash, so I followed his lead. We stayed there for about six months, saved money, and found a house. The deal was too good to pass up. The offer included two homes, that were side by side and a lot next to the end house. One of the homes was a six bedroom, one and a half bath and the other house contained three bedrooms with one bath. They were located on a quiet, secluded street. There were abandoned houses across the street and next to our homes that were set to be torn down. I viewed that as a huge opportunity to purchase the land around our home once the city demolished the properties. This was a very big accomplishment for me and Nate. We were a young, black, married couple, with four kids, who had just bought two homes with a lot for cash. I felt that we were winning, like we were making huge moves and would be on top of the world. Our life was one of a power couple. Both homes needed some work, so we continued to stay with his parents for about another three months while the work was getting done. I planned to get the smaller property renovated for my mom to live in so she could be close to her grandchildren and have a home where she did not have to pay rent.

During this time, I went back to school to obtain my Master's degree. I was trying to get pregnant and I was also planning our wedding. I had been at my job for six years and had the opportunity to go back to Pitt to obtain my Master's degree. My job had a program in which I could attend school full time, not work, but continue to receive ninety percent of my salary and keep my medical benefits. The only requirement was that I would have to maintain my employment with the agency for 16 months post degree.

The Master's program was very difficult. Although I did not work at my full-time job, I had an internship that I had to complete. Additionally, I had a second job where I would pick up time as I wanted to. Having four kids and needing to get our home fixed up so we could move, my main goal was to get my money up so we could do that. There was a lot of stress because of the responsibilities I had at that time. Class, school assignments, internship, being a mom, wife, ensuring that I attended school and extra-curricular activities, planning our wedding and working part-time put me into a space where I was continuously on the run and sleep was at a bare minimum.

My educational advisor did not ask, let alone

understand, what I was facing, but attempted to have me removed from the master's program. She stated that she was informed that I was unprofessional with one of the faculty members at the University. Now granted, I had gotten frustrated with one of the faculty members. The faculty member had called me and directed me to stop what I was doing and go and meet with my HR department to sign the contract, which was an obligation as my place of employment was paying for me to obtain my Master's. My frustration came about because I was at my internship and needed to accumulate enough hours each quarter and she was telling me to leave there and go sign the contract at that moment. I thought I had already signed the contract, but would come to find out that the contract I had signed was not the official contract, therefore it was necessary for me to go and sign this one. With everything going on in my life at the moment, I became a little frustrated, but didn't curse or say that I would not sign the contract. I actually left my internship and went and signed it. Therefore, that incident did not seem to be a reason to be put out of the program. Additionally, my educational advisor was required to meet with me once a quarter, but I failed to meet with her because the times that she scheduled were during the time that I was at my internship or in class. When I finally had the opportunity to meet with her, she was very unprofessional. I recall the meeting like it happened today. This woman had the audacity to look me in my face and ask, "What is wrong with you? You should be grateful to have the opportunity to be in this program. Given where you came from, many people wouldn't have this opportunity." She went on to say that she was going to ask for me to be put out of the program because my behavior was unacceptable. This took me totally caught off guard because I was attending all of my classes and there were no issues at my internship. Moreover, I was passing all of my classes with the required B or higher, so her wanting to put me out of the program for not meeting with her and because of a report she received left me confused. She told me that a meeting would occur and at that time I would be put out of the program.

I left that meeting bawling. I immediately called Nate when I got into my car and cried my eyes out to him. He told me that everything would be fine and he did not feel that I did anything to be put out of the program. He also encouraged me to speak with someone above her. I had worked hard to get to where I was in my life and for her to say what she did hurt me more than anything. She did not know what I was facing, nor even asked. She made me feel so small and like I really did not belong there; that it was a privilege to be a young black girl attending Pitt. No one at the

University ever made me feel like that and that would cause me to become stressed to the point that I had to start seeing a chiropractor because there was so much tension in my neck. This extreme stress led me to become short tempered with the kids. One day, I was rushing to get the older kids to the school bus and Jay to daycare, so I could get to class on time. None of the kids could find their shoes. I was beyond stressed because I wanted to get to class on time so that there was nothing additional held against me when we had the meeting. I found myself yelling at the top of my lungs at the kids because they had not put their shoes up when they came in the night before and that was going to make us all late. Nate's mom came to the top of the steps and asked me to come into her bedroom to talk to me. She bluntly stated, "You are an amazing mom to the kids and I never have anything bad to say about you, but they are young kids and you will not yell at them like that." Between my stressful life, school, me turning into a mom that I always dreaded, I most definitely felt the need to go back and try therapy. While in undergrad, and now in grad school, I educated myself in the behavioral health field so I would not continue to be ignorant to the fact that I was beyond stressed and needed outside help. I enrolled in therapy through a local church in my neighborhood but after a few sessions I stopped going. The therapist must have been new to the field, because she did not appear to understand my story. Additionally, her treatment delivery did not appear to be genuine and her delivery methods were straight from the book. During a session she even pulled out a book on mental health, asked me to read it, and asked me my thoughts about what I had read. I knew then that she was not a good fit for me, so I stopped attending. I attempted therapy prior to that experience, when Tink was approximately one. My job at the time, made me go to therapy, through an employee assistance program. I was the youngest person working there and so much gossip and backstabbing stuff was going on so I would cuss my co-workers out. HR felt that my actions were unprofessional and said that I had to attend EAP or I would be let go, so of course I went to therapy. The therapist to which I was assigned nodded off during a couple of my sessions. On one occasion, she briefly fell asleep. Both of my experiences with therapy had discouraged me from attending therapy ever again. Moreover, most times I was a good, patient, and nurturing parent to the kids, so honestly, I did not feel like therapy was necessary.

My advisor informed me of the meeting date, and I was quite afraid of the possible outcome. In the same breath, I felt that my advisor was beyond unprofessional. It showed during our meeting at her office, via the emails she sent me, and when she came to my internship to check in with me and my internship supervisor. The meeting at my internship went well, for the most part. The supervisor shared that I was doing extremely well and that there were no complaints. My advisor looked me in my face and out of nowhere she stated, "At least you know how to be professional here." My internship supervisor was lost because she had no clue about what was going on therefore, she inquired upon completion of the meeting. I told her what I was facing and she said that if I needed her to advocate for me at the meeting, she would do so, because she felt that what my advisor had just done was very unprofessional. I left that meeting feeling defeated because I wanted to go to the dean about the situation, but was afraid to because my advisor had been at the school for over twenty years and I felt that they would side with her. The Friday before the meeting, I found the courage to go and speak with the Dean because I felt that I was not being treated fairly. As I would catch the elevator to the twenty first floor, fear took over my body. My neck was beyond stiff because of the stress. The Dean was not in his office when I arrived, but the Associate Dean was. I was directed to her office to speak with her. Before a word could come out of my mouth, tears fell down my face. I had worked extremely hard to get to this place and I sat there defeated. I explained the situation to the

Associate Dean and she looked at me and said that she was going to make sure that I spoke with the Dean about it that day. She left her office and came back a few minutes later and shared that the Dean was in his office and wanted to talk to me. He said that he was just made aware of the situation and directed me to write down what had occurred and email it to him. He stated that he would be on campus tomorrow and would review my email then. He told me to have a good weekend and not to worry about the meeting on Monday. Even though he said that, I stressed the entire weekend. I felt my future was in the hands of my advisor.

Monday would arrive and the meeting was scheduled for that evening at 5 pm. I received an email from the director of the Master's program asking me to come and meet with her prior to the meeting because she wanted to attend on my behalf and advocate for me to remain in the program. Therefore, I made it a priority to meet with her prior to the meeting. She stated that she spoke with all of my professors and no one had anything negative to say about me. Moreover, I was passing all of my courses. The meeting was about to take place and I was prepared to express how I felt, that I was being treated unfairly. I had the emails, I had written down everything that occurred during our meeting and the meeting at my internship. I detailed the instance where she scheduled times to meet with me and I was unable to attend because of my internship or class. Moreover, the supervisor from my internship gave me her number so the school could call, if necessary. Upon arrival to the meeting, I walked in with the program director. She sat right next to me, kept me calm, and gave me tissues, as the tears raced down my face. The Director from my job, the supervisor from my job, and some of my undergraduate and graduate professors were there. I was surprised to see my undergraduate professors there, but they were present. My advisor shared her concerns and she was asking for me to be removed from the program. I had all of the evidence to prove my point, yet fear consumed me.

The supervisor from my job, basically in a professional manner, went off on my advisor, saying that he had been my supervisor for six years and had never seen the behavior that she was describing. He also stressed that this was a social work program, and helping me through the issues should be a priority, not putting me out of the program. He then asked what had been done to address the issues and crickets filled the room. The program director then mentioned that I was passing all of my courses and none of my professors had any concerns with my behaviors or professionalism. My undergraduate professors also stated that they too had never had any issues with me during my undergraduate experience.

No one but my advisor felt that I should be put out of the program. When the meeting did not go the way she had hoped, she attempted to say that she thought that the program was too much for me to attend full-time and suggested that I attend part-time. I did not agree with that, nor did my supervisor or anyone else in the room.

The meeting ended with me remaining in the program. I was asked, in front of her, if I felt comfortable with her remaining my advisor and with all of the support in the room, I stated that I did. After the meeting, I was informed that if I had any additional issues that I should bring them to the Dean immediately. After the meeting, as I sat in my truck crying, God spoke to me. He showed me the power that he had to slay any Goliath that came in my presence. God made it clear to never allow any individual or situation make me walk in fear ever again. What God has for me is for me and no person or situation can take it from me. From that day on I had no additional issues and my advisor treated me completely differently.

Tink's birthday came around and I surprised her and Nate's older son with a trip to tour the White House. They were both excited and happy about that. They were hoping to see President Obama and his family, but we did not have the pleasure of that. The first two years of Nate's and my relationship, we continued to travel frequently as a couple and as a family. Between family reunions, concerts, weekend getaways and taking the kids places for their birthdays, we were always hitting the road. I always wanted to show my kids the world and I made sure to plan things to do so.

A little over a month later, our wedding took place. It was beyond beautiful. It started off late, but the turnout was amazing. I had a big wedding party; ten men and ten women. Our four children were also in the wedding. I had the best makeup artist in the city do my makeup. Our theme was Winter Wonderland. We had a horse and carriage and the hall was set up beautifully. Tonya would help dress and prepare me for the ceremony. My foster mother, some of her children, and grandchildren attended my wedding. They remained supportive of me. My grandma did not attend, and my mom attended briefly. Approximately 150 guests attended and everyone appeared to have had an enjoyable time. I was in school, therefore we did not take a big vacation after the wedding but we did go to the Poconos.

Jay was around five and was ready to start kindergarten. I started to sign him up for different sports to see what he liked to do. He loved to play football and soccer. He was very little, so I did not allow him to play football that year, but soccer was a go. He also had a lot of energy and loved to run, so he also ran track with Tink. Jay had some behavioral issues and I was always on the phone with the school or at meetings advocating for his needs. I hated the fact that there were no schools for kids who had ADHD and the classroom was not equipped to teach children who suffered from being hyperactive. One thing that I did guarantee was that all of his educational needs were met on the level that he needed because that was the school's responsibility. At times I felt like I was being too hard on him, but at the same time, I did not want to lower my expectations of him. I wanted him to reach for the stars and expect the best of himself. My goal was for him to become a well-rounded, educated, black man, not a product of what society states.

With my auto-immune disorder I was having difficulty getting pregnant. I had gotten pregnant once, early in our relationship, but had suffered a miscarriage. After our wedding ceremony, we tried and tried to get pregnant, but were not successful. We had good medical coverage, so we went to the fertility clinic. Nate and I went through testing and were informed that it was unlikely that I'd get pregnant. They said that if I did, I would miscarry because of my auto-immune disorder. A couple of months later I did not get my period and found out that I was pregnant. Nate and I were both very excited. We went to our initial appointment, happy and taking all types of selfies. Since I was high risk, they wanted me to get a sonogram. While at the sonogram appointment, we were informed that the fetus was not developing correctly and that we needed to prepare ourselves for a miscarriage. I was approximately four months pregnant and was being informed to prepare to lose my baby. I broke down in the sonogram room and Nate comforted me. He said that everything would be ok and that we would have a baby. About a week later, which happened to be the day after Thanksgiving, Nate worked 6 am-2 pm and I was off that day. I woke up cramping and when I stood up out of the bed, the terror happened. I immediately called Nate. He rushed home and took me to the hospital. He was by my side through the entire process.

As I cried, he wiped my tears. As I would get on and off the toilet and as the clots hit the floor, he would clean them up. He cleaned me because I was not in the right state of mind to do it myself. After being at the hospital for a few hours, the bleeding slowed down, so we were sent home for me to continue to go through the process on my own. I was graduating with my Master's in a few weeks. I did not want to finish the program, nor attend graduation, but I did. On the last day to apply for graduation I received an email from my advisor reminding me to do so. It took everything in me to go to campus and apply. She emailed me late in the afternoon so I had to rush and get the kids from school, go to campus get a form completed by the School of Social Work, then rush to another part of the campus and apply for graduation. God was with me because I arrived at the registrar's office at 4:30 pm on the dot. The lady there happily processed my paperwork and told me that someone from the School of Social Work had called her and stated that I had my kids with me and that I was on my way over. She congratulated me and said that she was not going to leave until I arrived and she processed my paperwork. That made me find the strength to attend graduation. The day of graduation I cried all morning, while getting dressed, and after graduation about losing the baby. I tried to find joy in this accomplishment, but it was not joyous at all. At graduation I would have been about twenty weeks pregnant and I was going to announce my pregnancy to everyone. So not being able to do that was hard on me.

Upon completing grad school, I headed back to work. I was initially informed that I would be going back to the same office I was at before I started school. Just as I was sitting in class, waiting for the professor to arrive so I could take my last final, I received a call from my job. I was informed that I was to report to the intake office when I returned to work. I was livid because that was the last place I would have ever wished to work. I asked what had prompted the change and was informed that everyone that was returning from school was assigned to that office because it was very short staffed. I had so many thoughts about just quitting because my Master's degree would help me get hired almost anywhere. However, I loved the population of clients that I served so I stuck it out. I was placed under the most difficult supervisor. Several people had issues with her and they had been to HR about her.

About a week after graduation, we had planned to take the kids to Disney World for Christmas. I tried to find joy during the vacation, but I continued to cry daily about losing the baby. I really wanted the baby. The kids really enjoyed themselves. Nate and I decided to get tattoos with each other's names while in Florida. That evening was fun. He took me out to a local club near the resort and we had a blast that night. We brought my older nephew with us, so he could babysit when Nate and I went out. The kids had a blast at the parks and loved taking a helicopter tour. That was a trip that all of the kids would always remember. At this point, my relationship with Nate was growing and I really loved him. While in school, he held things down with the kids and worked two jobs. During the late nights, when I would be on campus studying, he would make sure the kids ate dinner and get them ready for bed. Sometimes he would even have their school clothes out for the next day. I would be moody at times, because my life was hectic, but he never disrespected me and was always humble when it came to me. I felt that he genuinely loved me. I felt, for once in my life, that I had met a hardworking guy, who took care of me and our children. I actually trusted him. I finally trusted a man. I never thought I would get to that point. Many times, he would come into the bedroom and see me crying about losing the baby and he would always promise me that we would have a baby together and tell me not to worry. Even though I strongly believed that Nate was my soulmate, I remained empty inside and the childhood pain and memories still consumed my heart, even though he was loving and kind.

Nate and I had purchased a timeshare when we went to the Poconos after we got married and Valentine's Day 2016, we planned a couple's trip through our timeshare. My two sisters came with their mates and three of Nate's friends and their girlfriends came. It was a total of six couples, so we rented three houses and two couples stayed in each house. All of the houses had two bedrooms, a den area where you could look down onto the entire second floor area, a full kitchen, dining room, fireplace, and hot tub. That weekend was one to remember. We drank, ate well, and had a ball the entire time.

147

We decided to drink and then go skiing. None of us could ski, so watching everyone fall was hilarious. We were constantly stared at because we were the only black people skiing. Nate and his friend decided that they would go to the top of the peak and snowboard down. That was an epic fail. We ended up seeing the motor skis bringing them down the slopes because they could not make it down. We played many games, went paint balling, went to Kalahari indoor water park, and all of the couples got massages.

Working for the supervisor I was under continued to be stressful. I went into her office one day to complete supervision and as we were going through my cases, she raised her voice and asked, "Didn't I tell you to do that last week? Why didn't you do it?" I looked at her, got up, and said, "I don't feel comfortable speaking with you any longer. I had to remove myself because I wanted to cuss her OUT. I got up and stated, "I am going to go and get the office director." She tried to change up and said that she would go and get the supervisor above her and she did. She returned with the office manager who was just as rude and not a people person. The office manager asked me what was going on and what I wanted her to do about it. I informed her of my supervisor's unprofessional behavior, which I experienced on various occasions. I then requested to be removed from her unit. The office manager responded, "I don't know if I can do that because every unit is full and I don't want to burden another supervisor by forcing them to be overstaffed." I left that meeting feeling rage in my chest. How the hell do you say I'm a burden, yet never addressed the unprofessional behavior of the supervisor? Thankfully, about a week later, I was moved to another supervisor's unit.

A couple of months later, I applied for a supervisor position and when I walked into the interview, I was surprised to find the regional office director, assistant office manager, and the supervisor I recently had the unprofessional encounter with, waiting to interview me. I put no effort into the interview because I thought it was a joke. How do you permit an individual who I just had a dispute with interview me? I should have advocated for myself and gone to Human Resources, but I applied for another position and thankfully, I was promoted out of that department anyway.

I continued to take the medication that my doctor had prescribed for my liver even though it did not make me feel right. I continued to get my monthly blood work done and yearly MRI, bone density scan, and endoscopy tests. Nate would always go with me for the endoscopy because I was put to sleep and had to have someone with me for the procedure. This time, he was tired from working, but he still attended with me. As I was prepped and an IV was put into my hand, he sat in the chair, knocked out. A pregnancy test was required prior to the procedure and who would have thought that my test would come back positive?! I was beyond happy and immediately woke Nate up and told him. He looked at me as if he was surprised, but did not appear happy. I do not know if that was because he had just been sleeping, but it was clear that he was not pleased. A month after that, things would change between us forever. A situation would occur at his parents' home, between one of Nate's family members and my child, and it basically put a wedge between us. This was the second time an incident like this occurred so this time I went ballistic. We could not come to a consensus about the situation and argued about it regularly. His children started to stay with his parents, instead of the home we shared. He would go between his parents' house and ours, but eventually, when I was around six months pregnant, he moved everything out of our home and went back to his parents' home for good. I was beyond crushed because I was pregnant and put in large amounts of time and dedication with his children. I even began to dislike his parents, because it appeared that they were minimizing the situation that had happened at their house. I felt abandoned once again. Pregnant and heartbroken, while trying to remain strong for

Tink and Jay. I enrolled Tink in therapy to be sure that she processed what had happened in a healthy manner. I was not going to minimize the situation, nor allow her to deal with it without seeing a professional. I was not going to allow what had happened with me to happen with my child. For about two months, every week, I accompanied her to her sessions. My heart was shattered as I felt like I failed my daughter and did not protect her. On the other hand, her therapist helped me to process what was happening and encouraged me not to blame myself for the situation. Moreover, she expressed how brave I was for ensuring that Tink received the proper help during this time.

The stress would continue. My family had our yearly family reunion and on our way to the reunion I got a call that James was there. That was the uncle who had sexually abused so many people in our family, as well as someone really close to me. When that person told me what he did, my uncle was in jail at the time, so I had not seen him up to that point. Therefore, my plan was to go and wreck the reunion because it was not ok for someone who had caused so much trauma to be permitted in an environment with so many people he had sexually abused. When I arrived, he was the first person I saw and I tried to fuck him up but he ran from me. My aunts and cousins tried to stop me, but I was so angry. My one aunt came over to me and I had rage in my eyes. I was pissed at her, because around this time, she was posting pictures of him on her Facebook page like he had not abused so many of her nieces. I was also pissed at my grandma because not only did she and my mom state that I was lying about the sexual abuse involving other people in our family, but also because she was all for him attending the reunion knowing what the hell he had done. Moreover, I was still hurt from her refusing to take me when I was in CYF care, as a teenager, especially since she took my brother and my two cousins. Therefore, when my aunt came over to me, I bluntly said, "Fuck him and Grandma. Fuck all of ya'll." I got in my car and left and did not attend another family reunion after that. I ended up talking to my aunt the next day about the situation. She was upset that I had said, "Fuck Grandma." I had to explain to her that she protected her kids from the sexual abuse and the shit he did was not cool, and grandma was co-signing his behavior. He should not be permitted around the people he had sexually abused, and he had never said that he was sorry or ever took responsibility for his actions. She told me that she understood, but deep down she was highly upset that I had yelled out, "Fuck Grandma." At that time, I was going through so much shit that I did not even care how anyone else felt because no one ever seemed to care about how I felt.

My grandma called me for about a month straight, leaving me voice messages saying that she was sorry. My mom called me one day saying that my grandma had been trying to get in contact with me. She said that my grandma had called her crying. My mom cried as well and begged me to call her, so I did. She was crying and said that she was sorry for everything. She wanted to know what she could do to earn my forgiveness, but I was going through so much at the time that there was nothing she could do. I told her that I forgave her, but at that moment I really did not; I just wanted her to stop crying. She continued to call me, asking to go out to eat or for me to come visit her. My schedule was crazy busy because Tink and Jay were always involved with extra-curricular activities and I always had two jobs. However, I did make time for us to go out to dinner together and she looked ill. She had difficulty breathing. She stated that she had stopped smoking but was still have issues with her breathing and she also had other medical issues going on. My grandma continued to try her best to build a bond with me, but I never put my guard down to allow that to happen because bitterness consumed me.

Nate came around here and there, but for the most part we were at odds during my pregnancy. He thought I was overreacting and that Tink did not need to attend therapy. He even attended one of the sessions and got upset after the therapist gave him an answer to one of the questions he asked and she provided a response he did not want to hear. He was partying all the time and hanging with his friends. He was also messing with other women during my pregnancy. During this time, anger and resentment began to fill my heart when it came to Nate. I started to really hate my husband. Like all I've done and showed you and your children, and this is what you do, leave your pregnant wife? I gave him many options for us to come to a consensus so our family could be back together, and he refused them all.

About a month before giving birth, we were on good terms and he was saying that he wanted to make things work between us. To be sure that I would be financially ok, I picked up work through a travel agency, to prepare for my three-month maternity leave, since Nate was no longer living at the house with me and my two kids. While working one of my shifts, Nate and I were texting and I asked him how he was going to bring in New Years'. Initially he joked. I then said that he needed to get himself together and work on his marriage. He then told me that he had not been the husband I needed him to be and that he had cheated on me basically our entire relationship. I immediately called him and asked him what the hell he was talking about. He told me that he had messed with five different women since being with me. One of them knew we were married but still messed with him. He stated that I would never find anything in his phone because he had another prepaid phone that he left at work in his locker. I asked him if there was anything else he wanted to tell me and he told me that he got a DNA test for another pregnancy around the time I found out I was pregnant. The little boy was three, almost four and his mother was a woman that he had messed with around the time he first met me. He stated that he knew the baby was not his because he used a condom with the girl but the girl insisted and took him to court and the DNA test came back that the child was not his. I asked him why he would wait until I was eight months pregnant to tell me this shit. He stated that it had been eating him up inside. He knew I had been loyal to him and his children and he felt bad. He said that he did not want to tell me, but it just came out, and he felt that I should know so I could make the decision to work through the issues with him or leave the marriage.

When you say heartbroken, I mean I was heartbroken. I was due to have our son in four weeks and got hit with this news. "Will the heartache ever end?" I asked myself. How much more pain and tragedy could one person endure? I ended up staying because I respected that he did come clean and felt that he was saying that he wanted to do and be better.

I had Samson a month after Nate broke the disturbing news to me. He picked me up the morning of my scheduled C-section. The delivery went well. My mom, Tonya, and Tink were all in the waiting room, anticipating Samson's arrival. They waited for hours, but I was high risk so no one was allowed in the room except for Nate, from pre-delivery to post-delivery.

I had to get a platelets transfusion prior to delivery because my platelets were very low and the doctors did not want me to bleed out. The C-section went well. Although Nate and I were not in a good space and did not even stay in the same house the night before, he smiled the entire time that morning. When Samson was taken out, Nate was the first person he saw. The doctors said that everything was perfectly fine with him except that he had six digits on each hand. I immediately panicked. Early in my pregnancy testing, the doctor called me, saying that he would be at high risk to have some malformations and blood disorders and he would not live over six months. However, the only issue he had was extra little fingers coming off the sides of his pinkies. Nate assured me everything was fine because Nate had the same thing when he was born.

Nate named him Samson. It was our plan that if it was

a boy, Nate would name him and if it was a girl, I would name her. The name had to be a biblical name though. I planned to name the baby Genesis if it was a girl. Nate named him Samson because Samson was one of the strongest people in the Bible. Moreover, Sampson's mother could not have children and it was only through God's will that she was able to conceive. Nate felt that our son had to be strong to make it because the doctors had said that I would miscarry and that I was also unable to get pregnant, so it was God's will to allow me to conceive.

While at the hospital, I cried daily. I did not want to be a single mother again. I got married to have a child with a husband that I would be with forever. I struggled emotionally and physically the entire time I was at the hospital. Nate had to bathe me because I could not do it myself. The most I could manage was to hold Samson and breastfeed him. Nate also took care of most of Samson's needs while at the hospital. I woke Nate up one night, crying that I wanted him to come back home. He stated that he would and after we were discharged, he did. He said that he too wanted to make our marriage work.

CHAPTER 12

Trauma is What Got Me Here

A bout a month after Samson was born, I started attending a church near our home. It was convenient to attend this church and the kids really liked it. I knew the Holy Spirit was really in this church because I felt it from the time I walked in, until the time I left. The people there would pray over me every time I attended and the prayers were working. I continued to cry daily, but it was only once a day instead of several times a day like it had been. Around this time, Nate and I also decided to go to marriage counseling to work through our issues. It took approximately three months to find a therapist that Nate felt that he could open up to. He was adamant about having a black therapist and preferably a male. I was finally able to locate Dr. Clarke and he was located close to our home and Nate's job. We scheduled our initial session and shared everything that was causing conflict within our marriage. Dr. Clarke made it clear that much work would need to be done and that we would need to come to a consensus about things. We had plenty to work on, especially the fact that Nate continued to dismiss the incidents that occurred at his parents' house. Nate said that he would do what was necessary for the marriage to work and that he was no longer messing with any other women. I explained that everything that was happening had me in a very unstable and emotional state because I cried daily since giving birth to our son.

Well, about a week and a half after our first therapy session, Nate laid passed out drunk in our bed. I made us something to eat and when I brought him his food, it was difficult to wake him up. Since he was totally drunk I asked him to open his phone and he did. I saw text messages that showed he remained involved with women before and after our therapy session, including the entire time I was pregnant with Samson. This took me to a very distraught state. Why would he come back home and attend therapy if he was continuing to live like he was not married? He was fully witnessing my distraught mental and emotional state and he continued to play with my heart. At that moment, I blacked out to the point that I acted in a manner that I never had before. I became violent with him. I had never allowed a man to take me to the point of being violent. He woke up to me punching him, throwing the plates of food at him, throwing everything on our dresser at him. I followed him in the hallway to fight him. I then followed him outside and busted the windows out of his car as he drove off. I had so much rage in me. So many guys had done me wrong and the one I finally thought I trusted did me the worst. He ran out and left me while I was pregnant, chasing other women. He really hurt me deeply, just like my mom did when she ran after that drug and my dad when he ran after that bottle. I could not take anymore. I took everything he owned and everything anyone in his family had purchased for us and I burned it. My front yard appeared to be a forest fire. My neighbor who lived up the street from me got so scared that he called the fire department. The fire department, police, and arson patrol came, and I made up a huge lie so I would not get arrested. All of this happened while my kids laid upstairs in their beds asleep. None of them woke up. The next morning, they asked what had happened and I made up another lie, but I think Tink knew exactly what had occurred even though she didn't mention it.

The rage within me towards Nate increased to such a high level because he did exactly what Delsin said he would do. I became pissed at myself because the entire time I was with Nate, I thought about Delsin, yet refused to contact him because of my relationship with Nate. I left Delsin alone when he was a huge support, my friend, and never lied to me about anything. He was the realest guy I came across. Why the fuck couldn't my husband be the same way?

I began individual therapy with Dr. Clarke, since working on my marriage did not seem to be possible with Nate's actions. Due to the situation that occurred at Nate's parent's home, I did not want Samson there because he could not speak for himself and they appeared not to take the situation that happened seriously. Nate respected my decision and would come to the house to see Samson. He also started staying with his friend and would take Samson there with him when he would get him. My bond with Samson was completely different from the one I had with Tink. I loved him, of course, but there were things that I did with Tink that I did not do with Samson. I went to all of Tink's medical appointments. However, when it came to Samson, Nate took him to a lot of his appointments. I also did not leave Tink overnight with anyone for the first year of her life. I found myself beyond stressed and did several weekend getaway trips. When Samson was not even six months old, over one Memorial Day weekend, I went to Vegas with my sisters, just to get peace of mind and get away from the stress I was facing.

That August, even though Nate and I were on the outs, we went to Jamaica together. We had paid for the trip a year prior because my cousin had planned the trip for his wife's 40th birthday. Several of my family members flew in and we had a blast. Given the status of Nate's and my relationship, we faked a connection throughout the trip, but we both felt the tension within our marriage. This was my second time to Jamaica and I made the best out of the trip. We stayed at an all-inclusive resort that had a night club and all types of activities for us to do. The food was amazing. We did a tour of Bob Marley's home, climbed Dunn's River Water Fall, went to a club off of the resort, and went to see the restaurant of the fastest man in the world.

Week after week I tried to figure out how the hell I was in this position. I had a good job, was educated, loyal, worked hard, took care of our home, took care of the kids' educational and extra- curricular activities and I found myself in a position where I was married, but a single mother once again. Why the fuck am I sitting in mental health treatment with everything I have going for myself? I bounced back from everything that I had endured in the past, how the hell did I get here? I had a Master's degree in this stuff so I should be able to treat myself, get better and bounce back. At least that's what I thought. On the other hand, my everyday emotions consisted of hurt, rage, anger, depression, and bitterness.

Dr. Clarke would help me to put things into perspective. The hurt, deception, lack of commitment and lack of loyalty from my husband is what triggered the emotional distress I was currently facing, but the root issues are what held me in captivity. The continuous trauma, childhood abandonment, sexual, physical, and emotional abuse, the lack of a parental attachment, unstable placements as a child, unhealthy relationships, unhealthy coping mechanisms, grief and loss, were the things that came to the surface as I continued to attend therapy. Throughout my therapeutic process, Dr. Clarke helped me process each of those areas so I could adequately heal. The dark place that I was in was beyond difficult to get out of. I could not bounce back like I had done in the past. I was stuck and could not fight through the state that I was in. This emotional pain took me to a mental state that I had never been in before. I really felt like I was losing my mind; like I was going mentally and emotionally crazy. This was the point where I knew I had to remain in therapy because I was fully aware that I was in a very unhealthy mental state. Moreover, I was educated enough to know, that to become fully whole, I needed to attend therapy to adequately heal.

I would bawl from the start to the end of every session

for about a year straight. As I attended sessions, week after week, giving him full details of every traumatic experience, Dr. Clarke helped me process everything and develop new habits. The weeping then turned into anger. I then went through a phase of hating and resenting Nate.

Dr. Clarke diligently worked with me through each phase of my grieving and treatment process. He made everything make sense, including explaining why I was in the state that I was in and how the trauma began when I was a child and the abandonment issues with my mom and dad resulted in me coping by smoking weed and looking for love in unhealthy relationships. My upbringing never modeled a healthy relationship and I was never really taught so I sought out what I thought was right. Dating older men was like seeking the father figure I never had and sadly, they all had ill intentions.

He showed me that I did not need to try to get back to the old Genafie. The old Genafie that I stated I wanted to get back to was not who I needed to get back to. He showed me that I needed to actually find out who Genafie actually is and to develop to become the best version of that Genafie. To live a full life and function at my best. We laughed during many sessions, but he was stern and upfront with me when needed.

During one of our sessions, I sat in front of Dr. Clarke, bawling my eyes out, and said, "I fucking hate feeling like this. I wish these feelings would just go away. I just want to be better. I'm tired of crying and being irritable." As he looked me in my eyes, he wholeheartedly stated, "Genafie stop being so hard on yourself. You have been through so much shit and it's going to take time for you to heal from everything that you have endured. You have not been in treatment a sufficient amount of time to deal with 32 years of trauma." At that moment, I did not want to hear that, I just wanted the time to come where I did not cry daily. He assured me that it would come, but only with time, patience, and hard work.

By graduating college and getting married, I thought I had broken the generational chains and was good, but so many childhood memories were laying silently dormant. As Dr. Clarke said, the pain and deceit from Nate just brought all of those traumatic experiences to the surface and I had to face all of them to fully heal. I attended therapy, but depression and anxiety continued to consume me. To be honest, I was most likely experiencing postpartum depression that was never diagnosed. I totally let myself go. I gained weight and did not care how I looked. I attended therapy, waiting for Nate to get his life together but he did not. I tried my best to keep it real with Nate during this time. I told him about wanting to see and write Delsin and I told him that the only reason I had not was because I was married. Earlier in our relationship, I told him that I felt bad for discontinuing communication with Delsin, because at the end of the day, he was a true friend and held me down during a huge time in my life. I knew communicating with Delsin during this difficult time would uplift and encourage me, but I did not give in because I was married. During that waiting period, attending therapy and going to church kept me half way sane.

At this point, it was a very difficult time in my life. While my role as a parent was important to me, always keeping it together was not easy. Tink would wake up and hear me crying and would ask me what was wrong. I would never tell her though. The kids just knew that Nate had done something married people should not do and at that time he would not be moving back with us. I tried to protect them because they had grown to love Nate. During Genafie's track season, I was extremely hard on her. I pressed her to compete better, but I didn't realize that Nate's absence, and her seeing me cry so often, was affecting her. I was also hard on Jay because he was getting calls home from school daily. It got to the point where I had to take him out of the private school and enroll him in our neighborhood school, which I dreaded. I permitted him to attend that school for a few months but he came home and told me that the teachers cussed often and a student's mother had come to the school and fought a teacher. After several stories, I took him out of the school and home schooled him. The following year, I enrolled him in a charter school. While at the private school and neighborhood school, the social workers spoke with me about putting him on medication, but I refused when he was in kindergarten and first grade. The end of second grade I had gotten him three different evaluations and was informed that he needed medication to be successful in school, therefore I permitted him to start medication. Once he started medication, I rarely received any calls home from the charter school.

I continued to struggle with depression and anxiety. In the past, I had always taken great care of my home, but during this time, things were in disarray. I was not keeping up with the laundry or cooking regularly. The kids ate out more often than I cooked. I became very irritable and moody and turned into someone that I dreaded.

The auto-immune medication side effects were also affecting my mental state and I was aware of this, but refused to take other medication to counteract the side effects. I did not take them while pregnant with Samson because I could not. My platelet levels remained low, but my liver levels were stable while pregnant, without being on any medications. The doctors were amazed because they thought that I would go into liver failure, since the baby really taxed my body while I was pregnant. Once I delivered, my liver levels elevated again and I was tired of all of the medications. Therefore, I started to look into holistic medication and found a woman whose daughter was diagnosed with this disorder. She wrote a book about healing her daughter after meeting a doctor in Mexico. I reached out to the lady and she gave me the doctor's information and the name of the natural medications her daughter was taking. I had a Facetime call with her, and she talked to me about a proper diet and not eating anything with dairy or gluten and to be sure that I took the natural supplements every day. She explained that I was not sick, but my body was toxic. The natural supplements would help take the toxins out my body. She said that the doctor in Mexico gave the natural supplements via IV for a week and then prescribed other meds upon completion of the IV injections. I started the natural medications and started feeling better than ever. I scheduled a time to see the doctor in Mexico but didn't actually need to go because my liver levels started to normalize.

With Nate no longer being there with us, it was hard on Tink and Jay because they both called him dad. Tink started asking about her biological father. One morning, she did not appear like herself. I asked her what was wrong and she started to cry. She stated that she felt that she did not have a dad now because Nate was like her dad and when he left, she stopped seeing him as much. She told me that she regularly cried herself to sleep at night because she felt that she was a good kid and did not understand why her real dad was not a part of her life. I explained to her that God has a purpose for everything and to pray for her dad and Nate. That triggered me to start reaching out to her dad, but he continued to say that he would get better and be a part of her life, yet he failed to do so. It had been almost five years since Genafie had last seen him. When he came to my house that day, about two weeks before Christmas 2013, I introduced him to Nate and that encounter must have stirred up some unwanted feelings for him because that would be the last time Genafie saw him and it was now fall 2018. All of 2018 I tried to get him to see her and to help with her needs but he did not and always seemed to have an excuse. He then told me that a real woman takes care of her kids without suing their father. I felt that I was a real woman long enough and it gotten me nowhere, so I got fed up and sued him. At the hearing, he walked in, saw me and asked me if I was ready for a DNA test. I looked at that fool and the anger began to manifest. Then, his girlfriend walked in and I went off. I asked him why the hell he would bring her to the child support hearing when she saw my daughter all of the time, with her kids, yet she did not speak to my child, so it made no sense for her to be there. I said, "I invited you all to Genafie's second birthday party and none of you attended, so why is she here now?" She tried to get smart and I went in on her. When it was time to speak with the child support staff, he changed his entire story. I said that I did not want anything from him until he got a DNA test. The child support staff stated that he signed the birth certificate and she asked him if he ever took care of Tink. He stated that he had, but not like he should have. She informed him that he could ask for this process to be put on hold and request to see the hearing officer to see if they would permit a DNA test. However, the hearing officer would probably deny it since Tink was now ten, he signed the birth certificate, and had taken care of her in the past. I told the lady that I wanted to request to see the hearing officer so a DNA test could be completed but she stated that the father would have to request it. This fool did all of that and did not even request to see the hearing officer. I was beyond pissed. After providing verification of Tink's school tuition, track, and competitive cheer fees, he was informed that her living expenses were $960 a month. Initially I was petty and stated that I wanted everything my daughter was entitled to. He continued to state that he could not afford that and the petty in me told him to have his girlfriend help him pay it since she wanted to come to court with him. After a while I put the pettiness to the side and settled for the amount that he said he could afford.

I saw my grandma again at her sister's 70th birthday party and she looked even sicker. Approximately a year had góne by since we had gone out to dinner. She could barely walk up the steps and breathing was extremely difficult for her. We had taken pictures that day and that was the first and only time she would see Samson. That following month, the day after Thanksgiving, I woke up to all of these missed calls from my Facebook messenger and from my mom and sister. I called my little sister back first and she said to call mom because she was saying that grandma had passed away. I called my mom and she told me that my grandma was found in her apartment, on the floor, dead. She stated that she was on her way to Pittsburgh and would see me soon. I rushed to my grandma's apartment, and saw her lying on the floor, next to the bed where she slept. Her headboard had a mirror with a little ledge where she would place things. As I looked, I observed Tink's hospital photo sitting right above the area where she laid her head each night. Between her grandchildren and great grandchildren, there were about ninety all together, so it touched me to see that out of all of the photos she could have had there, she had Tink's. It hurt my soul that I had not fully forgiven her prior to her passing. Seeing my baby girl's photo there made me realize that she loved me more than I thought and when she said she was sorry she actually meant it.

I would come to experience more grief and loss. When she first passed, I did not go to her grave, although it was near my home. I was hurt and sick that I let her pass without forgiving her. I never bothered to learn her history, to see what she had experienced, but I knew that the family dysfunction had been occurring for generations before mine. The thing about my gram was she actually had a life insurance policy and didn't leave any bills for the family to pay. I spoke at her funeral about forgiveness and encouraged my family to let gram's death be a way for a new beginning to take place. For us to start doing things differently and breaking generational curses so we could all heal.

Three months after my gram's death, I finally filed for a divorce. A month prior to filing, Samson had turned two and on his birthday Nate expressed that he wanted our marriage to work and would do anything including therapy and coming to a consensus about the situation that happened at his parents. At this point, it had been two years since Nate had disclosed all of his dirt to me. Additionally, he continued to live like we were not married and I was beyond fed up. Therefore, on my birthday I called him and asked him to come to the house and he did. When he arrived, I gave him the divorce paperwork. He willingly signed the papers but called me a few days later to tell me that he had bought me a ring and was going to give it to me on my birthday, but due to me having the divorce papers, he decided not to do so. I held onto the papers for about a month before I submitted them. Our divorce was then finalized three months later.

Throughout the previous two years, while I waited for Nate, I thought about Delsin often. He was my friend and I knew if he was home or if I could just hear his voice, he would uplift and encourage me though this difficult time, just like he did when I was pregnant with Tink. The crazy thing is, even though I knew Nate was messing with other women, I felt obligated to stay true to my marriage vows. Therefore, even though the thoughts of Delsin remained, I did not act on them. I felt that I would not allow Nate's actions to make me start doing things I should not do as a married individual.

Two months after the finalization, Nate texted me about taking our son to a cookout. He asked if I would be comfortable with Samson attending because his girlfriend would be there. I began to boil inside because I wanted to know how the hell a person has a girlfriend two months after getting a divorce. I kept my composure and said I was ok with it as long as Samson would be with him. When he signed the divorce papers, we had a conversation about meeting each other's partners once we began dating. Therefore, meeting her was a part of our agreement and Nate agreed for that to happen. He had no problem with me meeting her. However, that shit turned out to be a smack in the face, because he went from having a good wife and family to now dating a twenty-three-year-old woman. My first thoughts were, "Is she someone that is going to be around long term and should I allow Samson to be around her?" She didn't have any kids and Nate was 33, with three kids, and he couldn't have any more kids because he had gotten a vasectomy right after we had Samson. I bossed up, met her, and that motivated me to get my shit together and get to a healthy space. I refused to sit around in pity and stress about someone who had clearly moved on, not even three months after getting divorced. It was difficult, but I promised myself that this time I would get to know who I was and what my true purpose was. I promised to never again engage in a relationship that was not of God. From that point on, my full focus was on getting out of that depressive state and getting my mental state to a healthy place again.

As I started to build my relationship more and more with God, He would speak to me often through my kids. I tried to keep what was going on between Nate and me private and not involve the kids. Throughout the previous two years, Tink would help me so much around the house and with Samson. She would tell me how beautiful I was, and even when I reached a high of 206 pounds, she would adamantly express that I was not fat. If I was in my bedroom too long with the door shut, Tink and Jay would come in and check on me. Most times, they came in just to ask me what I was doing and to tell me that they loved me. I believe, although I was trying to keep what was occurring away from them, that they sensed something was not right about me. Jay's behavior in school was improving drastically. He was blowing my mind. One day he was given an assignment to write a poem. The teachers were all so taken by the poem because it was about how much he loved me. It was about how he was going to grow up and be someone so he could make a lot of money and take good care of me. And Samson was such a good baby. He rarely cried and was extremely healthy, smart, and very happy.

The presence of my kids made me sit down and really evaluate my mental state and realize that they deserved more from me. Those past two years I had been in a very dark, emotional state and was not always the parent I wanted to be for them. I was short tempered, yelled often, and my expectations of them became unrealistic. However, my kids were what kept me on my toes. They were always involved in extra-curricular activities and other than attending work, their events would be the only reason I left the house. I was tired of being in this dark place and often reminisced about the moment I found out I was pregnant with Tink. I promised that I would be the best mom and at the moment, I was not that. I came to the conclusion that I deserved to feel better, and my children deserved to see me in a better condition. I was continuing therapy and attending church, but more work needed to be done on my part and putting in that extra work to fully get through my current and past trauma became my primary focus. I made it my priority to work through every area that was hindering me from smiling, flourishing, and functioning at my fullest and healthiest state. I allowed working two jobs and my kids' activities to always consume all of my time and in turn, I never fully grieved nor worked through any of the trauma or hurtful past experiences. My past was eating me up internally and now it was showing physically. Going through a divorce put me in a space in which it forced me to deal with the demons that I had been suppressing; all of the childhood memories, the unhealthy relationships I had engaged in and the loss of loved ones. Getting a divorce broke me down but also provided the bricks to build me up again.

CHAPTER 13

Escaping bondage and finding a new way

The following year would consist of me focusing on going deeper in therapy and building a stronger relationship with God. This phase was extremely difficult, but I had to go through this period to get fully whole. Therapy was very beneficial, but my relationship with God is what helped me realize that I could not get through all of these traumatic events on my own. Therapy showed me that I never functioned in a healthy manner and I needed to become a whole new being. My spiritual walk guided me to flourish into that new being; into the Genafie that God destined me to be. God wanted me to evolve into an entirely new creature. He wanted me to put all abandonment issues, old patterns, behaviors, unhealthy ways of coping, hurt, pain, trauma, unhealthy relationships, and unforgiveness all behind me and I was determined to do so. God revealed to me that now was my time to shine my light into the dark places that consumed me and to become transformed and renewed.

During this time, God strategically placed a new spiritual family in my life. I had stopped attending the church that was near my home. There had been a change in pastors and leadership, approximately five times within the two years I was attending, and I did not feel the presence of the Holy Spirit within the church, as I did when I initially started attending. A young man named, Devantae Butler and his fiancée, at the time, were called by God to coordinate a bible study, via a Zoom call, and I decided to partake in it. Participating in that call had a significant impact on my walk with God and some spiritual breakthroughs that needed to occur.

Dr. Clarke began to really touch some areas that I did not wish to touch and held me accountable. Up to this point, I had tunnel vision when it came to how I viewed my past. I had allowed the devil's perspective of things to taint my mind, but with God on my side, the deeper we started to get during my therapy sessions, the more God started to speak to me and change my perspective on things.

When I was hard on myself or began to want to rush my healing process, Dr. Clarke brought that to my attention, and helped me refocus so I could finally get this thing called life in order. God also reminded me that this process would take some time and that he would continue to walk through it with me. As much as I wanted to rush my healing process, I learned that it was necessary for me to be in my current state, and it was not time for me to come out of it yet. I needed to allow God's completion to take place and while doing so, God restored me and gave me a strategy so I would never end up in this dark space again. This time around, God did not just want to break me free, but to set me free and allow me to undergo the full healing process. Therefore, I had to submit to the process and go through very difficult experiences and allow God to press those memories and thoughts out of me.

Through my new spiritual family and reading God's word, I became fully aware of the power of His word. Therefore, I started to create a flourishing atmosphere within the storm and refused to remain stagnant and conform to my circumstances.

On many occasions, Dr. Clarke would ask me questions and to avoid facing them, I would provide a response that did not answer what he asked. He, in turn, would gently and in a humorous way, let me know that I did not answer the immediate question and would walk me though getting to the core of things. He and God patiently walked me through each traumatic experience and as they did so, I started being released from the things that were holding me in bondage. My healing started with facing the core issue; the abandonment.

Abandonment

I lived life daily and did not realize the importance of how having healthy attachments in childhood played a role in how people functioned as an adult. In college, I learned about how the lack of healthy attachments and being abandoned by your parents, have long term negative effects on people. I, on the other hand, post undergrad, remained ignorant to the information. I did not feel that it pertained to me. I felt that I was fine because I graduated from college and had made it out of the struggle. However, I lived with inner feelings and displayed certain behaviors in every relationship that I entered. Dr. Clarke helped me to be cognizant of this and come to the realization that being abandoned by my parents had affected me and had been playing a major role in how I functioned as an adult. I had some serious mommy and daddy issues. To address them, Dr. Clarke had me write letters to both of my parents. God revealed to me that writing these letters was necessary to get through the rest of my trauma and to a new realm of life and that he would tenderly massage and nurture my heart and mind until I arrived there. God made it clear that he wanted me to live a life that I had never previously experienced, but I had to listen to Him and allow

Him to guide me, to prune the abandonment out of my heart because I could not do it on my own.

Remaining focused on the abandonment caused so much turmoil in my heart and resulted in me remaining stagnant for a long time and not being able to undergo the full healing that I needed. Fully surrendering to God, provided me a totally different perspective of the abandonment. He showed me that not only was He my heavenly father but had also been my earthly father. He reiterated the latter part of the scripture, Hebrews 13:5, "Daughter, I will never leave nor forsake you." I always felt that I endured so much because of my parents leaving me and God expressed to me that they may not have been there and may have left me, but that He had always been there.

The abandonment and lack of a loving attachment during my early childhood years caused a high level of anger, rage, bitterness, and malice in my heart. God, in turn, spoke to me through Ephesians 4:31, "Get rid of all bitterness, rage and anger, brawling and slander, along with every form of malice." This was difficult and on a daily basis I had to wholeheartedly ask God to fill me with the love Christ has for the church and within due time, He did. At this time, my mind became a battlefield. The more I fought, declared, and decreed for the abandonment issues to be pruned out my heart, the more Satan tried to use his tactics to keep me in bondage. Daily, I prayed and asked God to cover my mind and any thoughts that did not align up to His word.

The Abuse

The sexual, physical, emotional, and verbal abuse were next to be addressed. These issues were deep secrets for the most part, but secrets that were burning a hole in my heart, as well as consuming my mind. Although I had graduated with a Master's degree, one memory that would replay in my head over and over was the statement that my foster mother had said to me, "Bitch, you will never be shit." Another memory was my mom beating me with a bat and calling me a "Bitch" multiple times. And the many, many memories I had of fighting guys off of me. These memories made me feel worthless, insecure, and they played a major role in how I viewed myself and affected my self-esteem. Through God's word, the Holy Spirit started gassing me up, revealing to me who I am and whose I am. The Lord gave me 1 Peter 2:9, "But you are a chosen people, a royal priesthood, a holy nation, God's special possession, that you may declare the praises of him, who called you out of darkness into his wonderful light." This scripture spoke so much life into me. This showed me that I was not only royalty in God's eyes but I was also His special possession. Every negative thing that occurred or was said to me, I needed to put that underneath my feet because my father stated that I was special to Him. Everyone else left me in turmoil but He diligently picked me up out of this dark place and brought me to His wonderful light. Over and over He said how proud He was of me, even during the times that I felt like I was not living up to His standards. I began to train my mind to think of myself how God thinks of me and above all things, I am royalty to him. The memories remain, but they do not take over my mind and heart anymore. My every day walk consists of me knowing, wholeheartedly, that I am God's special possession.

Addiction

The abandonment and abuse resulted in me smoking weed and drinking at an early age. Even though, at this point in my life, the drinking and smoking had subsided, I still had addictive ways. To eliminate the chance of me or my kids ever lacking anything, I worked a lot. I became addicted to excessively working and always being busy. I became addicted to making money. I always maintained two jobs and a side hustle to make sure every need and want was met. Being broke was never an option for me. Working at the level that I was working became overwhelming, just as if I was out binge using for weeks at a time. It affected me physically, mentally, and spiritually. To be released from these addictive behaviors, I had to first be let loose from fear and learn to just trust God. I had to wholeheartedly grasp Philippians 4:19, "And my God will meet all your needs according to the riches of his glory in Christ Jesus." This scripture fed my soul and the more it was embedded in my spirit, the more I let go of fear, trusted God, and was released from my addictive behaviors. He gave me the strength to let go of the exhausting behaviors and helped me view things from a different perspective. God's help pulled me away from excessively working and everyday busyness and pushed me to trust Him and allow Him to provide for me and my children. Initially, this was challenging, because not working two jobs and being busy was abnormal to me. Once I fully grasped what God was telling me to do, He provided abundantly and exceeding for me and my children. We never went without anything and I mean anything. Through this season, God did some things that I would have never expected.

Unhealthy Relationships

With my educational background, I was fully aware that the unhealthy relationships that I found myself in stemmed from the abandonment and abuse that I had encountered. Therefore, once those two areas were addressed, refraining from such relationships became easy. Now, the attraction for street guys remained, but I was intelligent enough to know where such a relationship like that would go and did not engage in such. Moreover, I walked more confidently now. I walked daily, knowing that I was royalty, so I was no longer interested in partaking in unfulfilling relationships. I got to the point where I did not want a relationship based off of money, sex, looks, or one's status. God told me that my body was a temple and I was going to treat my body as such. I would no longer engage in a relationship that made me feel unworthy. Through God's word, He would mold me into becoming a Proverbs 31 women. He would also show me the type of man that was deserving of me. He spoke to me through Facebook one day, as I scrolled down my timeline. I saw a meme that stated, "A man who can give you everything but the love of Christ, will give you nothing at all." At that moment, God expressed that I could not submit to a man unless he had submitted to Christ. A man can give me the world, but if he cannot submit and love me like Christ loved the church, there is nothing he can do for me. God pushed me to strive for a man He knew I deserved, one that would help me experience love on another level, a love so deep that my spirit and my mate's spirit intertwined and I refused to submit to a man until that occurred.

Forgiveness

Forgiveness was the most challenging area I had to get through. I would say that I forgave people, but my behaviors would show differently. There was a list of individuals I had to find forgiveness for in my heart. This list included my mom, dad, grandmother, high school principal, Nate, Tink's dad, Aaron, and my one foster parent. To fully become a new Genafie and to be delivered, as difficult as it was, I had to wholeheartedly forgive others.

The letters that Dr. Clarke had me write to my mom and dad started the forgiveness progress. A breakthrough weekend gave me the opportunity and tools to break free from the bondage of unforgiveness. With regards to my mother's letter, Dr. Clarke suggested I give it to her, but I did not feel that she was in a space where she would accept responsibility for her actions and it would intensify the anger and hate I had towards her. Therefore, I never gave it to her, but I read the ten-page letter to Dr. Clarke about everything I felt. Most of the information expressed had been things she never knew I experienced or felt. My father's letter was much shorter; approximately three pages. It had now been fourteen years since he had passed away, and I sat tearfully, at his grave, reading that letter to him. While reading it, I felt the hurt, pain, and anger in my chest. Initially, I felt that writing the letters and getting everything off of my chest would be the key to my healing. Well, it was not. I had to fully release those feelings of hate and anger towards my parents to God.

As I read God's word, it stated that no matter what, I was to obey my mother and father and that I was to love and forgive, no matter what the issue is. Honestly, this was a huge pill for me to swallow because I really did not feel that they deserved my forgiveness. However, God would reveal to me that forgiving them is what was going to set me free. Someone once told me that unforgiveness is like drinking poison and expecting the other person to die. I was killing myself and my spirit by not forgiving them. Forgiving my parents was the hardest thing I had to do, but to become the new creation God called me to be, I had to do it. During therapy, I stated that I forgave them but my behaviors and inner feelings contradicted that. I needed a stronger source to help me prune those feelings of hate towards them out of my heart and the Holy Spirit did that. The more I grew with God, the more the Holy Spirit removed those feelings from my heart. It was not easy, and it took hard work and time. To help me with this process, God made me see my mom and dad in a different perspective. Through my prayers and petitions to the Lord, he created in me a new heart that I never thought I was capable to have. God told me to be appreciative of my mom; for me to be grateful that she was humble enough to call child welfare on herself once she realized her addiction put her in a state where she could not care for us. Many parents allow their kids to suffer while they are in their addiction, but my mom did not allow that. She called child protective services to get help and that resulted in us going to foster care. Moreover, my mom may have failed to do a lot of things but one thing she did not fail at was introducing me to Christ and that was the most important thing she could have ever done in my life. When it came to my father, God revealed that some people did not need to be a part of my life. He protected me from many people, including my dad. A relationship with him would have caused more harm than good. Looking at my parents, from God's perspective, helped me to be open to fully and wholeheartedly go through the forgiveness process. Now, I am at a place where memories and actions pertaining to my mom do not bother me anymore, nor do they make me upset. When I am in her company, I no longer cringe at the presence of her. Riding past my dad's grave use to trigger me to become angry but that does not have a hold on me anymore.

Forgiving my parents made it easier to forgive everyone else that I felt had hurt me. It revealed so much to me and drove me to look at every situation in a different perspective.

I was able to finally forgive my grandma for not taking me in and for stating that I was lying about the sexual abuse that I had disclosed to my mom. When it came to my grandma, Jeremiah 1:5 always came to mind. It reads, "Before you were formed, I knew you, before you were born, I set you apart." God set me apart, therefore, it was part of His plan for me not to live with my grandma. I would have taken another road if I had lived with my grandma. Therefore, I ought to be grateful that He set me apart and put me on the road that He did because I was able to accomplish so many things in my life that many have not been able to accomplish. Additionally, I have broken the generational curses of poverty, teenage pregnancy, abuse, addiction, and mental illness. Moreover, I am able to ensure that my kids have a healthy upbringing and do not ever endure the trauma I faced.

I refused to live a partial life anymore, so the forgiveness process continued. To help me stay on the road of forgiveness, I continued to make it a priority to look at each situation in a positive perspective. I was also able to forgive my one foster mom for the hurtful words that she said to me. Those hurtful words pushed me to become somebody and I am currently pursuing my educational dreams and in my second year of a doctoral of psychology program. My principal, by preventing me from walking at my high school graduation, showed me that there are things you should never say and that there is a consequence for my behaviors. Aaron, by being the first man to deceive me and break my heart, showed me that a man's actions speak louder than his words. After dealing with him, I never believed what a guy told me if their actions did not align with their words.

Tink's dad played a part too, by not being a part of her life. The fact that he lived within a few miles of our home, yet had not attempted to see her in five years, use to bother me. God revealed the same lesson that I had to learn about my dad. Tink is precious, God is protecting her and there are some people that do not need to be a part of her life. Therefore, it is ok that he is not involved because all of her needs are being met. Additionally, Nate may have not been the best husband, but he is a good dad and although we are divorced, he has remained a huge part of her life. Lastly, her dad's lack of involvement gave me the opportunity to explain the importance of prayer to Tink; to forgive and pray for him to become a better person and father one day. When I see him now, I can smile and my spirit is not moved by his presence.

My marriage with Nate revealed many things to me. First, to never do something that is not aligned with God's will. Nate was not to be permanent; he was not the husband

God had for me, but he was who I believed was to be my husband. Prior to meeting Nate, I wrote a list of what I wanted in a man and Nate fulfilled everything except two things on that list. See, with God's hands in things, he will fulfill every aspect and not have me compromise. Additionally, my list is not needed. God will reveal who he has for me and it is my responsibility to openly accept and be obedient the next time around. There also came a point when I was able to look at the hurt from Nate as a good thing. Through the pain he caused, I was able to face so many demons, traumatic thoughts, and feelings and become a new creation; become the Genafie that God destined me to be. I was finally living, not just surviving. I am now living a whole life; a life that I had never experienced in the past.

After forgiving all of the individuals that hurt me, I thought I was out the water, fully healed, and sanctified, but Dr. Clarke told me that I needed to finally forgive myself. I dealt with several men that were not worthy of me. I went through a phase in my life where I did not treat my body as a temple. More, frequently than not, I would drink and smoke in order to be intimate with the guys that I was dealing with. I had to forgive myself for allowing people who were not worthy of me to see and experience the intimate parts of my body. I had to forgive myself for defiling my temple. I had to forgive myself for not forgiving my grandma and Aaron before they died. After seeing my grandma laying lifeless on the floor; looking over and seeing Tink's baby photo right where she laid her head every night, it was distressing and painful to come to the realization of the abundance of love that she had for me. The fact that I did not forgive her before she passed away tore me up. The last conversation I had with Aaron haunted me. For many years, I walked around with the pain of knowing how mean and disrespectful I was to him not even an hour before he took his last breath. He had been gone for fourteen years, when I finally found the courage to go to his grave and ask for his forgiveness and to work through forgiving myself. My grandma and Aaron dying so suddenly showed me that tomorrow is not promised and no matter the situation, treat people like it will be your last encounter with them.

I thought past experiences were difficult, but this healing process was the most difficult thing I went through in my life. Having to relive and talk about all of the traumatic and hurtful experiences that I had endured was extremely challenging, but with God on my side, I fought through this overwhelming process. Many days I wanted to just say, "Fuck it," but something in me kept me attending therapy and building a stronger relationship with God. My life, up until this point, has continued to show me that I am a true warrior. I have been through so much, but I have always remained a true soldier through the battles and always fought MY way through every situation. I fought my way through the abandonment, abuse, hurt, pain, and losses. I fought my way through college, to be a better mom, and I fought my way out of poverty. I wholeheartedly fought through those battles. Prior to the divorce, I had taken each battle down, with my own strength, but I could not do that when faced with the divorce. The divorce knocked me clean out; it almost made me lose my mind. Emotionally fighting to get through that phase of my life was extremely exhausting and it made me come to the realization that the battle was not mine; actually none of the battles that I faced were mine to fight, they were God's. I can honestly say that God had to carry me though this last battle and while doing so, he healed and delivered me from all of the past trauma that I faced. As I would face, relive, and process each experience, God diligently held my hand, wiped every tear, and rubbed my back, assuring me that this too shall pass. During the times I was too weak to walk, God would throw me over his shoulder and diligently carry me through the wilderness.

God's love and grace has shown me who Genafie is. Genafie is more than a conqueror; the head and not the tail, above and not below; body is a temple and she is set free!! "Who the son sets free, is free indeed" (John 8:36). God clearly stated to me, "Never again walk in bondage, daughter!" God's love is so sufficient that I would never allow anything to hold me captive again!

I know my purpose now and it is my time to walk in my calling. I am going to continue to fight, but my fight will be to remain in alignment with God, His word and the calling over my life. Earthly battles I will no longer fight, as it is not my job to fight in that capacity anymore. Per God, "You fought many long and difficult battles, baby girl, now pass the baton to the spirit within you and from this point on, that is who forever will fight on your behalf."